ALEXANDER POPE

For Lawrence
With all good
wishes

6/4/09

Neil Curry

GREENWICH EXCHANGE
LONDON

Greenwich Exchange, London

First published in Great Britain 2008
All rights reserved

Alexander Pope © Neil Curry

Printed and bound by Q3 Digital/Litho, Loughborough
Tel: 01509 213456
Typesetting and Layout by EMK Services
Tel: 07990 950043
Cover design: December Publications, Belfast
Tel: 028 9028 6559

Cover image of Alexander Pope: © Mary Evans Picture Library

Greenwich Exchange Website: www.greenex.co.uk

ISBN 978-1-906075-23-1

Contents

1

The Pastorals **and** *Windsor-Forest*

Unless he is very gifted, and/or very lucky, a young poet can expect to have to work at his craft for many years, and to face many disappointments before he sees his poems in print, but Alexander Pope was not only outstandingly gifted, he also had the good fortune, at the age of 18, to attract the attention of Jacob Tonson, at that time the most influential publisher in England. Tonson, who had published both Milton and Dryden, wrote to Pope in April 1706 saying that he had seen one of his pastoral poems "which is extremely fine and is generally approved of by the best Judges in poetry", and offering to publish it in an anthology he was planning. Pope's career had begun and as it does so we notice that the old system of patronage is giving way to something new – to commerce. Pope, as will be seen, is to become the first fully-professional writer.

One lesson he still had to learn, however, is that publishers do not always hurry themselves and it was not until May 1709 that his *Pastorals* eventually made their first public appearance. But by this time – and he was still not yet 21 – his contribution had been extended to some two thousand lines. The one pastoral had become four, and the anthology now also featured a substantial piece translated from Homer's *Iliad*, together with free versions of Chaucer's *The Merchant's Tale*, and *The Wife of Bath's Prologue*. That these are two of Chaucer's more salacious tales perhaps makes them a not altogether surprising choice for a teenage poet to have made. He avoids the blatantly obscene – this is no longer Restoration England – but is risqué enough to catch the overall Chaucerian tone, and he certainly displays a sense of fun.

> He read how *Arius* to his Friend complain'd
> A fatal *Tree* was growing in his Land,
> On which three Wives successively had twin'd
> A sliding Noose, and waver'd in the Wind.
> Where grows this Plant (reply'd the Friend) oh where?
> For better Fruit did never Orchard bear;
> Give me some Slip of this most blissful Tree,
> And in my Garden planted it shall be!

In contrast, his Homer shows a decorum and solemnity befitting the epic, and when we read these translations we cannot help but be impressed by the skill which Pope already shows in his handling of the couplet – the variety of tone he can achieve in what would look to be such a restrictive verse form.

Skilful though the translations are, it was the *Pastorals* which caught the attention, as they were meant to do. This was how Virgil, Milton and Spencer had all begun their careers, and so was not only the accepted *apprenticeship*, it was also, one might say, a sign of serious ambition.

The pastoral is perhaps the literary convention we find most difficult to appreciate today: poets pretending to be shepherds, in turn pretending to be poets. It is so artificial as, frankly, to seem quite silly. But then, what of our own conventions? The dozens of television detective series we enjoy bear little enough relationship to reality, any more than did – and it is an interesting parallel – cowboy films. Conventions, I would suggest, are rather like bad habits: it is only those of other people we find obnoxious; our own don't disturb us at all.

In his essay *A Discourse on Pastoral Poetry* (written, he claimed, when he was 16) Pope suggests that keeping watch over flocks of sheep was probably one of mankind's earliest occupations, and so the songs those shepherds sang would have been among the very first poems. But, he argues, the writing of pastorals in his own day was more than simply an exercise in decorative nostalgia. There was a moral element to it. As the pastoral is "an image of what they call the Golden Age", so "an esteem for the virtues of [that] age might recommend them to the present." It is interesting to see such early signs of the moralist and satirist he was to become.

Pope's *Pastorals* were well received – one critic going so far as to claim "'Tis no flattery at all to say that Virgil had written nothing so good at his Age." And it was generally accepted that he had achieved what he himself had advocated in his *Discourse*: that the verse "should be the smoothest, the most easy and flowing imaginable."

As a unit the four poems show a high degree of organisation, following the cycle of human life and emotions as well as that of the days and the seasons: spring to winter; dawn to evening; joy to mourning. *Spring* is set at daybreak and takes the form of a contest between two shepherds singing the praises of their sweethearts. It does seem to be a Golden Age. They are young and happy and in love. All is equality and harmony, to such an extent that even their contest is declared a draw.

Pope had introduced a new element into the pastoral convention though. This is not the Classical world of the Mediterranean; this is England. Mount Helicon and the springs of Hippocrene have become Windsor and the River Thames. It is a patriotic poem, one might even say a political poem, being in its way a celebration of the House of Stuart: at its close the shepherds are heard asking each other riddles to which the answers are, firstly, the oak tree in which Charles II hid after the Battle of Worcester, and secondly, Queen Anne.

But as the sequence progresses, the Edenic Golden Age recedes and while the idealisation is still there, his shepherds are not spared the misfortunes and disappointments of normal life. In *Summer* it is now an unrequited love and the singer complains that " ... in my Breast the Serpent Love abides". When we come to *Autumn*, it is sunset. The birds "cease to sing", trees "fade", and "Lillies hang their heads and die." The two singers now have good cause to complain, as "This mourn'd a faithless, that an absent, Love." Momentarily, one of them even contemplates suicide. *Winter* is elegiac in every respect. It is dedicated "To The memory of Mrs Tempest", a lady who died with what has been called "grisly aptness" on the night of the Great Storm of 1703. The poem itself mourns the death of the shepherd's beloved and whereas Virgil's *Eclogues* had concluded with the triumph of Love, Pope's end with the triumph of destroying Time.

> But see, *Orion* sheds unwelcome Dews;
> Arise, the Pines a noxious Shade diffuse;
> Sharp *Boreas* blows, and Nature feels Decay,
> Time conquers All, and we must Time obey.
>   (85-8)

I have said that Pope's *Pastorals* were well received, but not by everybody. Thomas Tickell, encouraged in all probability by Joseph Addison, an influential critic whose friendship with Pope was always at best uncertain, wrote a series of five 'anonymous' essays in *The Guardian*, praising a rival pastoral sequence by Ambrose Philips, and ignoring Pope totally. None too pleased, Pope managed to deceive the editor by submitting a sixth essay, again anonymous, in which he

3

appeared to be deriding his own work and praising Philips. But whatever he praised him for, the supporting quotations were ludicrous proof to the contrary. For instance, having extolled Philips' elegance and beautiful rusticity of language, he backs it up with:

> Ah me, the while! ah me, the luckless day!
> Ah luckless lad, the rather might I say;

Philips, understandably, was incensed, and kept a birch at Button's Coffee House, where Addison and his friends used to meet, threatening to whip Pope with it if he ever dared to enter. But Pope had won. He had even coined a nickname so devastating for Philips – *Namby-Pamby* – that it has stuck in the language. Alexander Pope was not only a skilful poet, he was also a skilled literary strategist.

While Pope's next substantial work was *An Essay On Criticism*, it seems logical to leap-frog over this briefly and say something about his *Windsor-Forest*, which, if not a pastoral, is certainly a rural poem and was partly written at the same time as the *Pastorals*.

Pope's family moved to Windsor when he was 12 years old. He had been born on 21st May 1688 in London, in Plough Court, off Lombard Street where his father, who had converted to Roman Catholicism, was a prosperous linen merchant. But 1688 was also the year in which the Catholic James II had been forced to flee the country and William of Orange had landed in Torquay with an army of 140,000 Protestant troops. It was not a good time to be a Catholic and especially not one with the family surname of Pope! Mobs attacked and destroyed Catholic churches and the new administration was soon passing discriminatory laws through parliament, including one which prohibited Catholics from living within ten miles of the City centre. Pope's father can never have expected to be able to carry on trading with any degree of success in such a hostile atmosphere, but now he found himself obliged to leave. After selling the business, however, he retired with £10,000 – some say £20,000; either way it was a fortune in 18th-century terms, and he was able to buy a small manor house set in 19 acres of grounds in Binfield in Buckinghamshire, an area where several well-to-do Catholic families had already established themselves. Pope grew up there, the bookish, only son of elderly parents, and as a university education was, thanks to another government decree, closed to Catholics, it can be said that from the age of 12 he seems to have educated himself. He was by no means a solitary youth though. On his visits to London he was, despite his age, quickly accepted by the literary set which met at Will's Coffee House, where John Dryden had once held sway. What always seems strange to me is that he was not only befriended, but supported there by writers and critics thirty and forty years his senior, among them being William Walsh, whom Dryden had called "the best critic of our nation", the celebrated dramatist, William Wycherley, who had written *The Country Wife*, and the poet and Jacobite politician, George Granville, Baron Lansdowne, to whom Pope was later to dedicate *Windsor-Forest*.

Granville was one of the 12 Tory politicians elevated to the peerage by Queen Anne in 1711 in order to establish a majority in the House and so ensure the ratification of the Treaty of Utrecht, a treaty which brought an end to the long-running war with France. The closing section of *Windsor-Forest* can be read as a celebration of that Treaty, but it is not the way the poem had begun. In fact there had been a break of possibly seven or eight years between the *original* poem, written at the same time as the *Pastorals*, and the final third.

The poem may have begun as a 'landscape poem', following the example set famously by Sir John Denham in 1642 with his *Cooper's Hill*, but such poems were not merely descriptions; they were meditations. As Pope wrote of *Cooper's Hill*, " … the description of place, and images raised by the poet, are still tending to some hint, or leading into some reflection upon moral life or political institutions." And the closer we look at this poem, the clearer the political element becomes.

Windsor Forest was a Royal Forest – a hunting preserve – which means that, as well as trees, its 100,000 acres included meadows, farmland and rough moorland and the *painterly* way in which the opening section sets this varied scene for us clearly owes something to the fact that when in London Pope used to stay with the painter Charles Jervas and for a while was taking daily lessons from him. But the view with which we are presented is not only scenic, it is also thematic. In its blend of opposites – hills and vales, woods and plains, earth and water – *Windsor-Forest* represents what was known as *concordia discors*, the belief that ordered variety or harmonious confusion was the governing principle behind the universe as a whole, the balance which is achieved by the tension existing between opposites. It is, as Pope explains, a landscape

> Where Order in Variety we see,
> And where, tho' all things differ, all agree.
>
> (15-16)

Seen in this light, Windsor Forest is both a place and a principle, a poetic symbol for a world in which harmony prevails and so, as one would expect, it has that idealised quality of 18th-century landscape, but Pope then goes further and claims that nothing can surpass it – neither the glories of Classical Greece nor the gorgeous exoticisms of the distant East. And all this, he insists, is thanks to Queen Anne – "Peace and Plenty tell, a STUART reigns."

In contrast there follows an unexpected and what at first seems a somewhat exaggerated account of the brutalities inflicted on the area in Norman times by William the Conqueror. Unexpected, that is, until we realise that it is a thinly-veiled attack on another William – William of Orange, and his Whig supporters. Did William of Orange have any right to rule, other than that of conquest? The question is implied, if not openly asked. His reign was seen by the Tories as an interruption to the Stuart succession. His oppressive laws were regarded as tyrannical and he was blamed for starting the War of Spanish Succession which was aimed at preventing the Spanish empire from falling into the hands of France, a war which the Treaty of Utrecht was about to bring to a close. Early versions of the poem had contained lines as explicit as

> Oh may no more a foreign Master's Rage
> With Wrongs yet Legal, curse a future Age!

But as the arrival of the Hanoverians seemed more and more likely, they were wisely cut out. The account of the Normans concludes with the death of William II in a hunting accident. That William of Orange had also died as a result of a hunting accident only a decade before is not openly mentioned, but can hardly have escaped the notice of Pope's readers, if they were in need of any further prompting. William's horse had caught its foot in a molehill and thrown him, for which Jacobites would drink a health to "The Little Gentleman in Velvet" for many years to come.

Under Queen Anne, however, hunting was more democratic and not a totally royal prerogative and the following section celebrates the yearly cycle of hunting scenes in a sequence of vignettes as lively and as brightly coloured as in any medieval manuscript. In autumn young men go ranging through the woods and over the hills shooting pheasants and netting partridges. In winter the wildfowlers are out after woodcocks and lapwings. In spring "The patient Fisher takes his silent Stand" and when summer comes round again it is time to be up and away on horseback, with hounds baying after the deer.

These scenes allow Pope to introduce Diana, goddess of the hunt and of chastity and to tell the story of Lodona, one of her virgin attendants, who was pursued by the lustful god Pan, but saved in true Ovidian fashion by being transformed into a stream just as he was about to catch her. The Loddon is a tributary of the Thames and

> Still bears the Name the hapless Virgin bore,
> And bathes the Forest where she rang'd before.
> (207-8)

The principle of opposites, or 'Order in Variety' allows Pope to move from the activity of hunting to the tranquillity of the meditative life and after some lines in praise of the Thames, he changes direction and introduces the 'Happy the Man' theme, made famous by the Roman poet Horace. The 'Happy Man' who, in this instance, leaves the city and the court to enjoy a contented rural retirement, as the theme demands, is Sir William Trumball, a politician who gave up public life and became a neighbour of the poet's family at Binfield, where he enjoyed "Successive Study, Exercise and Ease" and would often go out riding through the countryside with the young Alexander. From politics to poetry, and Pope now recalls four poets especially associated with Windsor: "Majestik Denham", author of *Cooper's Hill*; Abraham Cowley; Henry Howard, Earl of Surrey, the 'father of the sonnet' and the first English poet to use blank verse; and of course his friend Granville.

From poets he moves to a list of kings buried at Windsor: Edward III; Henry VI, the 'Martyr-King'; Edward IV and Charles I. It was the execution of Charles, he suggests, which brought about such divine punishments as the Civil War, The Plague and the Fire of London, until – and in a conscious echoing of the words of the Bible:

> At length great ANNA said: 'Let Discord cease!'
> She said, the World obey'd, and all was *Peace!*
> (327-8)

At this, the River God, "Old father Thames", rises up, attended by all his tributaries and hails the "Sacred *Peace*" which the Treaty of Utrecht is about to introduce. In tones of triumph he foresees London joined with Westminster and becoming the greatest city and port in the world, its navy establishing an empire which would bring peace, prosperity and liberty to all and put an end to such evils as Discord, Terror, Ambition, Vengeance, Persecution, Faction and Rebellion.

It is, quite evidently, the heralding of a new Golden Age. Of course, it was not to be. It never is. Queen Anne died the year after the poem was published and the German House of Hanover arrived to take control. The Tory party fell from power and the Whigs impeached Granville, imprisoning him in The Tower along with the Tory leader, the Earl of Oxford. They also impeached Pope's close friend, Viscount Bolingbroke, but he fled to France and joined the Court of the Pretender. Then in 1715 came the disastrous Jacobite Rebellion. From Pope's perspective it had all gone wrong and gone wrong so quickly, but the exuberant idealism and youthful optimism of *Windsor-Forest* needs to be kept in mind as it helps to explain the disillusionment of his later *Satires* and the bitterness of *The Dunciad*.

2

An Essay on Criticism

In May 1711, when Pope's *An Essay on Criticism* was first published, his name was not on the title page. This was probably a wise decision as it is not difficult to imagine how literary London would have reacted to being told how best to do its job by a youth of 23, who had so far published no more than a handful of pastorals, accomplished though they might be, and a few translations in one of Jacob Tonson's *Miscellanies*. But, being anonymous, the poem was judged on its merit; Addison calling it "a masterpiece of its kind". Years later Johnson gave it as his opinion that "… if he had written nothing else, it would have placed him among the first critics and the first poets, as it exhibits every mode of excellence that can embellish or dignify didactic composition."

And the time was right for it too. After the audacious freedoms enjoyed and exploited by English poets in the first half of the 17th century, the need was beginning to be felt for the establishment of some accepted literary criteria, and not only in the writing of poetry but also in the criticism of it. In France there had recently been a spate of such criticism, and from some of their leading poets, including Boileau and Le Bossu, but the tone of it was prescriptive, dogmatic and rule-bound in a way which was not at all to English taste. It smacked of tyranny and so was looked down upon as being typically French. Yet, at the same time, it was felt that criticism in England was getting out of hand, as can be seen from the sequence of definitions Johnson's *Dictionary* gives for the word *Critick*: " (1) A man skilled in the art of judging of literature; a man able to distinguish the faults and beauties of writing; (2) An examiner; a judge; (3) a snarler, a carper, a caviller; (4) A censurer, a man apt to find faults." One explanation, in Addison's view, for this state of affairs, being that, "As there are none more ambitious of fame than those who are conversant in poetry, it is very natural for such as have not succeeded in it to depreciate the works of those who have."

Clearly something needed to be done, and recalling more amicable times when "The gen'rous Critick fann'd the Poet's Fire",

(Line 100) Pope's aim in his *Essay* was to find some middle course between authority and anarchy, while trying to reconcile creativity and judgement, and literature and criticism. His opening lines, however, show where he thought the problem lay, and it wasn't with the poets:

> 'Tis hard to say, if greater Want of Skill
> Appear in Writing or in Judging ill;
> But, of the two, less dangerous is th' Offence,
> To tire our Patience, than mis-lead our Sense.
>
> (1-4)

Granting that *True Taste* in a critic is as rare as *True Genius* in a poet, but arguing that "Most have the Seeds of Judgment in their Mind", (Line 20) his suggestion is:

> First follow NATURE, and your Judgment frame
> By her just Standard, which is still the same:
>
> (68-9)

Nature has always been a difficult word to define with any certainty, so varied are its uses, but in this context it appears to mean the essence of things, whatever is universal and unchanging and which all men can agree upon. And in terms of writing, he argues, it is to be found in those works of Classical literature which have survived for many hundreds of years. Their survival must mean, logically, that they possess some inherently lasting qualities, and it is these qualities, these 'Rules' which need to be studied closely and followed:

> *You* then whose Judgment the right Course wou'd steer,
> Know well each ANCIENT's proper *Character*:
>
> (118-9)

he says, and then adds:

> Learn hence for Ancient Rules a just Esteem;
> To copy Nature is to copy them.
>
> (139-40)

He is not, of course, advocating simple, slavish imitation. What he is saying is that it is up to each new generation to seek to *assimilate* those qualities which enabled ancient writers to give such eloquent voice to the concerns of our common humanity, and because of which they are still able to speak so clearly and forcefully to us today.

In the second section of the poem (Lines 201-559) Pope outlines the "Causes hindering a true Judgement", causes including Pride, Envy, Partiality, Prejudice and so on. It has to be said that many of the issues raised in this section, while by no means irrelevant, do not hold our attention quite so closely today. What does hold our attention – seizes hold of it in fact – is the quality of the poem as poetry, for after recounting the dangers of Pride, Pope begins the next paragraph with "A little learning is a dang'rous Thing", a line we instantly recognise, a line which we seem to have known for ever. And it is not alone. Next to Shakespeare, perhaps no other poet has written so many lines which have entered our linguistic consciousness with the force of proverb. Over the next few pages we meet with "To Err is Human, to Forgive, Divine" (Line 525) and are told that "Fools rush in where Angels fear to tread." (Line 625)

Incisiveness of this kind is what Pope's favoured medium, the enclosed or heroic couplet, not only encourages but demands. The couplet was not new, of course. It dates back to the 14th century and Chaucer's *Canterbury Tales*, but it had been given its Augustan polish and perfection by John Dryden. In a conversation with his friend Joseph Spence, Pope once confided that he had "learned versification wholly from Dryden's works." But not everyone thought so highly of rhyme. In Dryden's own lifetime John Milton had spoken out against "that troublesome and modern bondage of rhyme." In his preface to *Paradise Lost* he dismissed rhyme as "trivial and of no true musical delight" and "the invention of a barbarous age, to set off wretched matter and lame metre." Strong words, but Pope managed to explain them away by suggesting that blank verse would not have worked even for Milton except that "his subject turned on such strange out-of-the-world-things as it does." So much for the Fall of Man.

The couplet needs to be seen as a natural reaction against the complexities, and especially the stanzaic complexities of the metaphysical poets of the early 17th century. It is its very opposite: the nearest thing in its day, one might suggest, to "the language really used by men." It was also perfect for the aims which Pope has set himself. Its pairs of verses invite contrast and comparison, and hence analysis. It is not a medium suited to introspection or in which to express personal emotion, hence it largely disappeared from the scene during the Romantic Period. Its strengths are precision and lucidity and the exactness of disciplined thought.

Now a great deal of thought had gone into *An Essay on Criticism*. Pope was extremely well-read in the subject, both the modern texts and the ancient, but it needs to be remembered that this is not a treatise or a prose tract. There is absolutely no doubt that he could have written such a thing, had he wished, but this is a *poem*. We also need to bear in mind the contemporary understanding of the word *Essay*. It did not, as it does today, suggest the kind of learned article which might be submitted to an academic journal. Johnson defines it as "A loose sally of the mind; an irregular, indigested piece; not a regular ordered composition." Viewed in this light it should not surprise us at all when Pope slides from a consideration of the "Causes hindering a true Judgement" into a virtuoso demonstration of his own poetic skills:

> But most by Numbers judge a Poet's Song:
> And smooth or rough, with them, is right or wrong:
> In the bright Muse tho' thousand Charms conspire,
> Her Voice is all these tuneful Fools admire,
> Who haunt Parnassus but to please their Ear,
> Not mend their Minds; as some to Church repair,
> Not for the Doctrine, but the Musick there.
> These Equal Syllables alone require,
> Tho' oft the Ear the open Vowels tire,
> While Expletives their feeble Aid do join,
> And ten low Words oft creep in one dull Line,
> While they ring round the same unvary'd Chimes,
> With sure Returns of still expected Rhymes.
> Where-e'er you find *the cooling Western Breeze*,
> In the next Line, it *whispers through the Trees*;
> If *Chrystal Streams with pleasing Murmurs creep*,
> The Reader's threaten'd (not in vain) with *Sleep*.
> Then, at the last, and only Couplet fraught
> With some unmeaning Thing they call a *Thought*,
> A needless Alexandrine ends the Song,
> That like a wounded Snake drags its slow length along.
> (337-57)

In that simile which we can all recognise – going to church to join in the singing not to listen to the sermon – Pope first points a finger at those critics who only pay attention to the sound of the verse and ignore what is being said. *Numbers*, at that time, meant *rhythm*, and in a subtle change of direction of which we are hardly aware, we find him listing, and at the same time skilfully demonstrating, the various nastinesses which are to be heard in shoddy verse. In line 345 it is our own ears which are assailed by a succession of *open vowels*. In the next line there is indeed one of those feeble and useless *expletives* (auxiliary verbs) *do*; and this is followed by a brilliant line of ten dull monosyllabic words creeping along like mice.

(It perhaps needs to be pointed out, as we are about to look at rhyme, that in Pope's day *join* and *line* were perfect rhymes; it is our pronunciation of *join* which has changed.)

As it is the couplet which is under consideration, something has to be said about rhyme – in this instance poor rhyme. If we go back to Pope's fourth pastoral, *Winter*, and look at lines 61-2, we will find that he himself was guilty of rhyming *Breeze/Trees*, but he got away with it there. Here he manages to make it sound silly as its appearance is telegraphed long before its arrival. The cheeky parenthesis in the next couplet, where after *creep*, the reader is threatened (not in vain) with *sleep* is, I think, a tour de force quite beyond comment.

The couplet is built up of two ten-syllable, five-stressed (usually iambic) lines, but there had been a fashion of introducing, by way of variety, a twelve-syllable line, known as an *Alexandrine*. To Pope's ear it was not only unnecessary, but far too long and he proves it with an Alexandrine of his own, slowly dragging it out while at the same time giving us an image of a wounded snake!

Having shown us what not to do, Pope was not afraid to go one step further and demonstrate how it ought to be done:

> 'Tis not enough no Harshness gives Offence,
> The Sound must seem an Echo to the Sense.
> Soft is the Strain when Zephyr gently blows,
> And the smooth Stream in smoother Numbers flows;
> But when loud Surges lash the sounding Shore,
> The hoarse, rough Verse shou'd like the Torrent roar.
> When Ajax strives, some Rock's vast Weight to throw,
> The Line too labours, and the Words move slow;
> Not so, when swift Camilla scours the Plain,
> Flies o'er th'unbending Corn, and skims along the Main.
> (364-72)

Of all the outstanding verbal skills on display here, those in the

Ajax couplet seem to me the most remarkable. It is not that it is a tongue-twister – nothing so commonplace – but that there is a genuinely physical effort involved in moving your tongue and lips from the shape required to pronounce the 'X' sound of *Ajax* to the 'V' sound in *strives*, and once you have managed it, you immediately have to do exactly the same thing once again with *Rocks* and *vast*. The line does not only involve, it demands *labour*, while the long vowels of *strives*, *vast*, *Weight* and *throw* ensure that the words do *move slow*, and the effect is then emphasised by the contrasting couplet which follows, where it seems impossible not to exclaim it as swiftly as Camilla herself as she "skims along the Main". Again Pope is not only stating a point, but demonstrating it to us at the same time, and that, "*The Sound must seem an Echo to the Sense*" has since become a maxim in practical criticism courses everywhere.

Part III is headed 'Rules for the Conduct of Manners in a Critic', an unexpected criterion, but Pope insists that:

> 'Tis not enough, Taste, Judgement, Learning, join;
> In all you speak, let Truth and Candor shine:
>
> (562-3)

He goes on to encourage Modesty, Good-Breeding and Sincerity and then advances, in a series of rhetorical questions, what he considers to be the "Character of a good Critic":

> But where's the Man, who Counsel can bestow,
> Still pleas'd to teach, and yet not proud to know?
> Unbiass'd, or by Favour or by Spite;
> Not dully prepossest, nor blindly right;
> Tho' Learn'd, well-bred; and tho' well-bred, sincere;
> Modestly bold, and Humanly severe?
>
> (631-6)

Once, but it was long ago, he tells us, there were such critics and this leads him into a brief history of criticism from Aristotle and Horace, who "charms with graceful Negligence" (line 653), through Petronius and Longinus, then through the Dark Ages when "Monks finish'd what the Goths begun" (line 692), until he reaches his own contemporaries, ending with a warm tribute to William Walsh, "the clearest Head, and the sincerest Heart". (line 732) Although Dryden, as I have already observed, considered Walsh "the best critic of our nation", he is remembered now only for the advice he once gave to

14

Pope. "When I was about fifteen," Pope told Spence, "I got acquainted with Mr Walsh. He encouraged me much and used to tell me that there was one way left of excelling, for though we had had several great poets, we never had any one great poet that was *correct* – and he desired me to make that my study and aim."

Exactly what Walsh meant by that has never been totally clear, but what is certain is that throughout his life Pope revised and revised his drafts until he was absolutely satisfied, so that now it seems impossible to change a syllable without destroying everything, and while the intellectual content of *An Essay on Criticism* may not be new and may not be challenging, one can apply Pope's own words to it and say:

> True Wit is Nature to Advantage drest,
> What oft was Thought, but ne'er so well Exprest.
> (297-8)

There was, however, one flourish of his wit – in today's sense of the word – which was to have a lasting effect on his life. Among his strictures against poor criticism there is a brief aside on one particular critic:

> But Appius reddens at each Word you speak,
> And stares, *Tremendous*! with a threatening Eye,
> Like some fierce Tyrant in Old Tapestry!
> (585-7)

And that was John Dennis – easily identifiable at the time as he was the author of a tragedy, *Appius and Virginia*, which had been a flop, and one of his favourite, and over-used words was *Tremendous*.

Dennis has been called the "antitype of everything the *Essay* proposed", but then Pope was surely guilty of violating his own stated standards: this was certainly not an example of 'good manners'. What Dennis had done to upset Pope we do not know, but what we do know is that Dennis was a man with a high opinion of himself and a very short temper – he had been sent down from Cambridge for stabbing a fellow student – and it took him only a very short time to publish a pamphlet, *Reflections, Critical and Satyrical, upon a Rhapsody called an Essay upon Criticism*, 32 pages of criticism and personal abuse. Dennis was an able critic and had some significant points to make, but it was the poet not the poem he was aiming to get. And Pope was an easy target.

A portrait of Pope at the age of seven shows a bright-eyed, chubby-cheeked child, healthy and robust, but then when he was 12 he contracted tuberculosis of the spine, Pott's Disease, probably from infected milk. It stunted his growth and gave him a very marked hunched back. Dennis knew what to aim for and had no hesitation. "As there is no creature in Nature so venomous, there is nothing so stupid and so impotent as a hunched-back toad." And there was more – 32 more pages of it. One might say that Pope had asked for it, but Dennis had only opened the door. Abuse of this nature was to be thrown at Pope for the rest of his life; not, as we shall see, that he wasn't more than able to take care of himself in this kind of literary warfare.

3

The Rape of the Lock

Rich young people with time on their hands are always liable to get up to something silly. And at a party in the late autumn of 1711, 23-year-old Robert, Lord Petre did just that: he cut off a lock of Miss Arabella Fermor's hair. She, understandably, was furious, and so was her family. Indeed, as the families of both young people were of some social standing in a very close-knit Roman Catholic community, the fall-out threatened to escalate and become a "dire event", so Pope was asked by his friend John Caryll if he could write something to "laugh them together again". And he did. There was no personal motive for him in doing so. It is very unlikely that he was acquainted with either family. In fact by the time the second (1714) version of the poem appeared, Lord Petre had not only married someone else, he had died of smallpox. But neither event seems to have concerned Pope; his literary instinct told him that the situation was ripe with potential. What he wrote was his most brilliant and famous poem, *The Rape of the Lock*.

Arabella Fermor, it has to be said, did not immediately see the funny side of it, but when the second version of the poem sold some three thousand copies within four days of publication, she was not slow to relish the fame it brought her.

Looking at the story as it is told in the first edition of 1712, we read of Belinda (as the heroine is called in the poem) waking up one sunny morning and setting off with her friends by boat to Hampton Court where they laugh and gossip, play cards and indulge in the new fashion of drinking coffee. It is then that the villain (simply called the Baron) cuts off the lock of Belinda's hair. There is instant uproar and among all the shouting and fighting the lock somehow gets lost. It has, it seems, been gathered up into the heavens and become a new constellation, thus making Belinda's name not only famous but immortal.

Stated thus baldly, it is hard to believe that there is enough substance here to support a poem of any significance and indeed the first version ran to only two cantos, little more than two hundred lines, and is not all that remarkable. But the following year, when Pope declared his intention of translating *The Iliad*, he seems to have realised the *full* potential of what he had before him – the possibility of combining the 18th century's two favourite literary genres: the epic and satire, so that the later version, the one we read today, runs to five cantos, is more than three times as long as its predecessor, and is the most accomplished *mock-epic* in the English language.

The *mock-epic*, it must be understood, does not in any way mock the epic. The epic's position as the most prestigious of all literary forms was unassailable, and certainly not open to mockery. Dryden had called it, " … the greatest Work which the Soul of Man is capable to perform." What the *mock-epic* does is to take a story or a situation which is already silly and trivial and then to relate it in epic terms so that the contrast, the laughable inappropriateness of it, makes the situation appear even sillier than it was in the first place. There is also, however, a strong moral purpose behind the *mock-epic* in that it can be seen to contrast the nobility of mankind as it had once been with what it has since become.

We also need to be clear about what Pope and his contemporaries meant by the word *epic*, as today an accumulated vagueness surrounds it, so much so that in general usage it has come to be little more than a synonym for *big* or *important* and is applied to anything from a boxing match to a film which simply happens to have a lot of people in it. As a precise literary term, size and importance are still significant elements: an epic is a very long narrative poem and deals with matters of national consequence such as dynastic wars and the founding of nations. There is also a definite grandeur to it, to its attitude, language and style, but there are also a number of events and situations common to the works of Homer and Virgil and it is chiefly by means of these that we are able to identify and define the word when it is used in a literary context.

The central figures of such a poem, the heroes, were always men – military men, leaders – and the fates of nations depended on their deeds of derring-do. Great battles were therefore an essential feature as were the celebratory feasts. Other features common to both Homer and Virgil were the account of a visit to the underworld and of course the part played in all these events by the gods, by Zeus, Hera, and Pallas Athene, for example, who, motivated by the very human and un-heroic weaknesses of lust, envy and hatred, would frequently intervene in the action.

Now already we can see how very non-epic Pope's story is. The central character is not a military hero, but a girl. What happens to her is hardly of national importance. There are squabbles instead of battles and the great feasts are reduced to a coffee morning. We have only to conjure up a mental picture of men's fashions during the first half of the 18th century – the wigs, the tight stockings and the silver-buckled shoes – to be very aware that it was not, at least among the aristocracy, a macho society. Furthermore, in the 1712 version of the poem, two elements are missing: no underworld and no gods. Pope was able to rectify this when he came to re-write it, but not without difficulty. How could the gods be introduced to a contemporary situation? Any inclusion of the Christian deities would be looked upon as a blasphemy quite beyond question, and particularly from a poet known to be a Roman Catholic. And the pagan gods of the Greeks and Romans would look oddly conspicuous, not to say ridiculous, were they to be shown walking along Piccadilly or the Strand. How Pope overcame this problem is, as we shall see, one of the poem's outstanding achievements.

Before considering the text however, something needs to be said about the word *Rape* in the title. A lock of hair cannot possibly be *raped* in the way we commonly use the word, but it can be, and was, *carried away*, which is what the Latin word *rapere* means and from which it is derived. In the story of *The Rape of the Sabine Women* they were carried away and that is exactly what is happening in Poussin's famous painting. No doubt they were raped later, but they were carried away first.

But to put the event into perspective, if today you were to fondle or even touch the lock of a woman's hair, it would be construed as sexual harassment and could cause you a lot of trouble. To cut it off would be a gross violation and possibly a criminal act. So of course there is a deliberate sexual ambiguity in Pope's title. In *The Iliad* Homer recounted the battles of the Trojan War; here we have the age-old Battle of the Sexes, and sexuality, overt as well as covert, is a constant motif throughout the entire poem.

*   *   *   *   *

There seems to be something in the human psyche which tends to make readers skip Introductions, but the *Dedicatory Letter to Mrs Arabella Fermor* (Mrs was also used at that time for unmarried women) which prefaces *The Rape of the Lock* is not as casual, nor as inconsequential as it might at first appear. In its second sentence Pope claims that his poem "was intended only to divert a few young Ladies, who have good sense and good humour enough to laugh not only at their sex's little unguarded follies, but at their own." It is, of course, the lack of these two virtues which has been the cause of all the family quarrels and they are, in consequence, the very positives which the poem is about to advocate. In the closing Canto, one of Belinda's friends tries to make her see the "dire event" for what it really is.

> How vain are all these Glories, all our Pains,
> Unless good Sense preserve what Beauty gains.
>
> (V, 15-6)

Belinda, still incensed, rejects such a notion out of hand, but the reader is not meant to.

Pope then goes on to confess to Arabella that the first version was hurriedly written and even incomplete as it lacked "The Machinery": i.e. the gods. He explains to her, "The Machinery, Madam, is a term invented by the Critics, to signify that part which the Deities, Angels, or Dæmons are made to act in a Poem: For the ancient Poets are in one respect like many modern Ladies; let an action be never so trivial in itself, they always make it appear of the utmost importance." This is, considered carefully, rather a patronising and cheeky explanation in that it is telling her that she has made far too much out of something that is really quite trivial, but he concludes with a delicate compliment, assuring Arabella that all the characters in the poem are fictitious and that Belinda "resembles you in nothing but in Beauty". But the word *trivial* appears again in the first two lines of the poem.

> What dire Offence from am'rous Causes springs,
> What mighty Contests rise from trivial Things
> I sing –

Readers familiar, as Pope could expect them to be, with Dryden's translation of the opening lines of *The Aeneid*:

> Arms and the Man, I sing, who forc'd by Fate
> And haughty Juno's unrelenting Hate,
> Expell'd and exil'd, left the Trojan Shore

or Pope's own *Iliad*:

> Achilles' Wrath, to Greece the direful Spring,
> Of Woes unnumber'd, heavenly Goddess, sing!

would recognise this as the standard invocation with which epics begin. And of course it is true that "am'rous Causes" and "trivial Things" – Achilles' sulk and the abduction of Helen – did give rise to the "mighty Contests" of the Trojan War.

But it is trivia which occupies most of the succeeding lines. Instead of a world of heroes, we are in 18th-century London, the *beau monde*, with its idle young Lords and coquettish Belles, where the "mighty Rage" we are told, is not the prerogative of soldiers, but "in soft Bosoms dwells". Throughout the poem we will see Pope switching from one mode to another in an instant – within a single couplet – the sudden juxtaposition of opposites serving to highlight the satirical picture of society he is aiming to present.

To a lesser extent Pope can also be seen to be mocking the language and the attitudes of conventional Romance, so that when we first meet with Belinda she is just waking up, as all sleepless lovers do – at noon! She has, it seems, been having a rather erotic dream "That ev'n in Slumber caus'd her Cheek to glow", and before she is fully awake her "guardian Sylph" whispers a warning in her ear. He begins by explaining to her – and therefore also to us – what exactly sylphs are. Pope had already indicated briefly in his preface that the 'gods' in his poem were a race of diminutive beings, who, according to a bizarre religious sect called the Rosicrucians, inhabited the four Elements of Earth, Air, Fire and Water.

This particular, and seemingly bi-sexual, Sylph, by the name of Ariel, tells Belinda that she is not simply waited on by the maids, servants and footmen she sees around her every day, but is attended by "a thousand bright Inhabitants of Air". These beings, he says, were once women just like her, with vanities and idiosyncrasies just like her, and in the after-life were accorded a 'rank' appropriate to how they had lived their lives. So that a Termagant – vividly defined by Johnson as "a brawling turbulent woman" – would become a

21

Salamander and live in Fire. Gentle, more accommodating girls, were *Water-Nymphs*, while Prudes sank down to the Earth again and became troublesome *Gnomes*. Ariel, rather like Belinda herself, had been a flirtatious coquette and so was a *Sylph*.

> The light Coquettes in *Sylphs* aloft repair,
> And sport and flutter in the Fields of Air.
>
> (65-6)

Sylphs, Ariel goes on to recount, act as guardians to young girls, keeping their virtue safe "at Courtly Balls, and Midnight Masquerades ... when kind Occasion prompts their warm Desires." At first glance this all sounds very warm and friendly, but what Ariel is in fact saying is far from flattering. People may think that it is a well-bred young lady's own sense of honour that prevents her from getting into trouble, but not so:

> 'Tis but their Sylph, the wise Celestials know,
> Tho' *Honour* is the Word with Men below.
>
> (77-8)

We are only half-way into the First canto, but already the moral standards of this society are looking somewhat ambiguous. Is the glittering surface no more than a charade? It certainly looks like a marriage-market where, from the woman's point of view, the men are not men, but commodities, to be judged by their material value. It is a market place where:

> ... Peers and Dukes, and all their sweeping Train,
> And Garters, Stars, and Coronets appear,
>
> (84-5)

and where the girls are taught to advertise their own assets by painting their faces and fluttering their eyelashes.

Having explained all this – largely for our benefit – Ariel announces that he has come chiefly to warn Belinda of some impending "dire event". He is not sure what it is, but she must be careful. "Beware of all," he says, "but most beware of Man!"

But Belinda is no sooner properly awake than her eyes light upon a love-letter and once she has read that she forgets everything she has been told. It is time to go out on the town; time to put on her own make-up.

One standard feature of an epic is *the arming of the hero*, and in the lines which follow Ariel's speech we have the poem's first substantial parody, when Belinda, it may be said, puts on her own war-paint.

> And now, unveil'd, the Toilet stands display'd,
> Each Silver Vase in mystic Order laid.
> First, rob'd in White, the Nymph intent adores,
> With Head uncover'd, the Cosmetic Pow'rs.
> A heav'nly Image in the Glass appears,
> To that she bends, to that her Eyes she rears;
> Th' inferior Priestess, at her Altar's side,
> Trembling, begins the sacred Rites of Pride.
>
> (121-8)

It would not be only Pope's Roman Catholic readers who would recognise the sacrilege implied here: the silver vases she keeps her cosmetics in on her dressing table seem to mimic the chalice and paten on an altar. But more than that, the lines are saturated with religious vocabulary: *unveil'd, mystic, adores, heav'nly image, Priestess, altar, sacred rites.* Clearly some sort of religious rite, some sort of worship is going on here, and when we read "To that she bends, to that her Eyes she rears", we realise that Belinda is worshipping not only herself, which would be vanity enough, but an *image* of herself, the appearance rather than the reality.

The full "sacred Rites of Pride" (a Deadly Sin of course) then begin. The extent of the pride is seen in the exaggerations which follow, but there is also an element of social and economic criticism implied in them, in that they seem to acknowledge the international plunder that goes on to support such vanity and extravagance and to provide the "glitt'ring spoil". The gems are from India, the perfumes from Arabia. There is even what we would recognise today as ecological exploitation.

> The Tortoise here and Elephant unite,
> Transform'd to Combs, the speckled, and the white.
>
> (135-6)

But it is the famous line "Puffs, Powders, Patches, Bibles, Billet-doux" which points to the confusion, not to say perversion of values in the life she leads, where love letters and Bibles are of equal importance among the jumble of her dressing-table.

Canto II opens with an extravagant burst of imagery to describe

Belinda setting off to sail down the Thames to Hampton Court with her friends. She is the centre of attention; such is her beauty, all the young men are looking at her. In the previous Canto it was her vanity and frivolity we had been made aware of, but it is vanity, pride and frivolity in general the satire is aimed at, not solely Belinda herself. In the role she is expected to play she is equally a victim of the marriage-market mentality. The poem is not, as I see it, anti-women. Pope manages to make us recognise Belinda's essential innocence and to sympathise with her vulnerability. In an elegant and charming couplet he says:

> If to her Share some Female Errors fall,
> Look on her Face and you'll forget 'em all.
>
> (17-8)

And this might be the moment to emphasise how frequent and meticulous were Pope's revisions. In the first version the line had read "you'll forgive 'em all". *Forgive*? No, it's not a question of forgiveness. But *forget* is perfect.

One of Belinda's most beautiful features was her hair – especially those ill-fated locks or ringlets, and the Baron has decided, in language recalling Caesar's *veni, vidi, vici*, that he will have one of them.

> He saw, he wish'd, and to the Prize aspir'd.
>
> (30)

Just as an epic hero would (and Belinda did) ceremoniously put on his armour, so he would then (as the Baron does now) pray to his gods for victory. But in the Baron's case, his altar is built of "twelve vast French Romances" and the offerings on it are, revealingly:

> ... three Garters, half a Pair of Gloves,
> And all the Trophies of his former Loves.
>
> (39-40)

He prayed, "Soon to obtain, and long possess the Prize". But whatever his gods were, they were as fickle as he and only listened to half of what he said. He would never, as we will see, manage to keep his trophy.

Meanwhile, Ariel's anxiety is growing ever stronger and he

summons all Belinda's attendant sylphs to a meeting, strongly reminiscent of Satan's address to the assembled devils in *Paradise Lost*. He is still unsure what will happen and in the way he expresses his doubts we again see how the couplet was the ideal medium for satire.

> Whether the Nymph shall break *Diana's* Law,
> Or some frail *China* Jar receive a Flaw,
> Or stain her Honour, or her new Brocade,
> Forget her Pray'rs, or miss a Masquerade,
> Or lose her Heart or Necklace at a Ball;
> Or whether Heav'n has doom'd that *Shock* must fall.
>
> (105-110)

Diana was the goddess of chastity, so for Belinda to break her law would be to lose her virginity, but by putting it in the same couplet and so in the same context as a frail China jar, Pope is equating the two, suggesting that they are equally fragile and maybe of equal importance as far as Belinda is concerned. The same effect is achieved in the next line but in a different way: the same verb *stain* governs (in rhetoric this is called *zeugma*) two different objects – *honour* and *brocade* which ought to be of very different value, but seemingly are not. The contrasting balance of opposites in the next two lines suggest that her *Pray'rs* are a *Masquerade*, and that she might lose her heart as easily as she might lose a necklace. But worse than any of these possibilities, the final line seems to be saying, is the thought that her pet dog *Shock* might die. Now that would be serious and Ariel decides that he himself must guard *Shock*.

Pope was writing for a highly literate audience. The written word provided much of their entertainment as well as information, and so he could expect his readers to be familiar with the tradition in which he was working and to recognise the echoes and parallels with other literary texts. Certainly one of the pleasures of reading this poem has always been the slight intellectual frisson to be had from remembering, for instance, Satan's thunderous roll-call of the titles of the assembled devils in *Paradise Lost*:

> Thrones, Dominations, Princedoms, Virtues, Powers

when we hear Ariel calling his diminutive troops together with the words:

> Ye Sylphs and Sylphids, to your Chief give Ear,
> Fays, Fairies, Genii, Elves and Dæmons hear!
> (73-4)

And realising that there were seven layers of material in Belinda's petticoat because in *The Iliad* Ajax had seven layers of leather in his great shield. The petticoat, however, has not always, we are told, proved to be defence enough.

> Oft have we known that sev'n-fold Fence to fail,
> Tho' stiff with Hoops, and arm'd with Ribs of Whale.
> (119-120)

The *whalebone* of ladies' corsetry has suddenly become a whole rib!

Ariel warns his troops that they need to be extra vigilant and threatens them with terrible punishments should they neglect their duties, and diminutive though they are, there is a kind of terror to them which we can sense, even if we do not know the exact parallels without the aid of footnotes.

> Whatever Spirit, careless of his Charge,
> His Post neglects, or leaves the Fair at large,
> Shall feel sharp Vengeance soon o'ertake his Sins,
> Be stopt in Vials, or transfixt with Pins;
> Or plung'd in Lakes of bitter Washes lie,
> Or wedg'd whole Ages in a Bodkin's Eye:
> Gums and Pomatums shall his Flight restrain,
> While clog'd he beats his silken Wings in vain.
> (123-130)

The sounds in that last line can be heard brilliantly re-creating the frustrated effort and doing exactly what Pope had advocated in the *Essay on Criticism* when he insisted that "The Sound must seem an Echo to the Sense."

Meanwhile, Belinda, oblivious to all the commotion going on around her has arrived at Hampton Court and after some gossip with her friends, sits down to play a game of cards with the Baron and an unnamed third player. The game they play is *Ombre* and Pope's account of it is, to my mind, an astonishingly brilliant achievement.

In his praise of *The Rape of the Lock* Samuel Johnson had written that in it, "New things are made familiar, and familiar things made new." The sylphs were new to us but by this time we are quite at ease with them and now we are about to be shown a game of cards in a totally new light.

To have seen that the great battles of the epic tradition could be reduced to, and represented by, a game of cards was an insightful and imaginative step, but Pope took the idea several strides further. The Kings and Queens and Knaves seem to step off their pasteboards and become active, living beings, but at the same time Pope looks at the faces of the cards and points to a tradition which I had not previously been aware of: that each of the Kings has a beard; each Queen carries a flower and each Knave a halberd in his hand. But beyond that, he shows us that only the King of Clubs holds an orb and that only the King of Diamonds is shown in profile. Familiar things are indeed made new.

In a line with decidedly Biblical echoes, "'Let Spades be Trumps!' she said, and Trumps they were" and the game then begins. Each player has nine cards and while Belinda wins the first four tricks and looks certain of victory, the Baron wins the next four and she is suddenly facing defeat. But the last trick goes to her.

Pope has not been content to generalise about the game. He is specific and in fifty (47-98) lines describes each hand so clearly that it is possible to replay the game in its entirety, as follows. (Some of the trump cards have individual names.)

Belinda		Baron		A.N. Other
✓	A_ (Spadillio)	3_		4_
✓	2_ (Manillio)	5_		6_
✓	A_ (Basto)	7_		3_
✓	K_	J_		J_
	K_	✓	Q_	5_
	6_	✓	K_	4_
	4_	✓	Q_	5_
	Q_	✓	J_	6_
✓	K_	A_		6_

Belinda was ecstatic.

The Nymph exulting fills with Shouts the Sky;
The Walls, the Woods, and long Canals reply.
(99-100)

She must have made quite a noise if it echoed so far outside and John Dennis, in one of his more pompous and humourless moments demanded to know, " ... is Shouting and Roaring proper for a well-bred Lady?" No, she is clearly, he says, "an arrant Ramp."

Pope obviously does not think so, but in lines which would not have been out of place in a true epic, a note of warning is struck.

> Oh thoughtless Mortals! ever blind to Fate,
> Too soon dejected, and too soon elate!
> Sudden, these Honours shall be snatch'd away,
> And curs'd for ever this Victorious Day.
>
> (101-104)

The game over, they all settle down to drink coffee, an event described for us in such exaggerated terms that when it is poured into the cup we are told that, "China's Earth receives the smoking Tyde".

But it is at this moment that the Baron, armed with a pair of scissors (variously described as a *two-edged weapon*, a *little engine*, and a *glitt'ring forfex*) generously lent to him by one of Belinda's 'friends', cuts off the lock.

> Then flash'd the living Lightning from her Eyes,
> And Screams of Horror rend th'affrighted Skies.
> Not louder shrieks to pitying Heav'n are cast,
> When Husbands or when Lap-dogs breathe their last.
>
> (155-8)

The action seems to freeze at this moment while a Gnome (they had once been prudes) called *Umbriel* descends into the *Cave of Spleen* – the poem's equivalent of the epic's descent into the Underworld. The spleen is actually the organ in our bodies which destroys defective blood cells, but in ancient medicine it was held to control one of the four 'humours', black bile, and so was associated with melancholy and fits of anger, and in Pope's own day was held to be responsible for female 'moods'. Hence the Goddess of Spleen lies on her bed protected by attendants called *Pain* and ('I've got a headache, dear') *Megrim*, or migraine, together with *Ill-Nature* and *Affectation*. Pope paints a positively Gothic scene for us with *glaring fiends* and *gaping tombs*. It has been called a "limbo of sexual and social frustrations" and there is something weirdly Hogarthian about the list of "bodies chang'd to various forms by *Spleen*":

Here living Tea-pots stand, one Arm held out,
One bent; the Handle this, and that the Spout.
(49-50)

In a footnote Pope says these are not entirely inventions, but certainly "And Maids turn'd Bottles call aloud for Corks" is a line as blatantly sexual as hardly to qualify even as a *double entendre*.

Umbriel's aim in going down to the *Cave of Spleen* was to ask the Goddess for her help.

Hear me, and touch *Belinda* with Chagrin:
That single Act gives half the World the Spleen.
(77-8)

He lays his credentials before her: he had "rumpled petticoats" and "tumbled beds" and "caus'd suspicion when no soul was rude" and so just as Odysseus had been given a bag containing all the adverse winds which might have threatened him, so she gives Umbriel a bag full of sighs and sobs and a vial full of tears. Back he goes, bursts the bag over the heads of Belinda and her friends and then the rumpus really starts, but what seems to concern Thalestris most is not so much what has happened, but what people will *say*.

How shall I, then, your helpless Fame defend?
'Twill then be Infamy to seem your Friend!
(111-2)

So much for honour and so much for friendship; this is a very fragile and fickle society where reputation is all.

Thalestris demands that her friend, Sir Plume, do something about it, but men never merit a good mention in this poem and he lives up to his name.

(Sir *Plume*, of Amber Snuff-box justly vain,
And the nice Conduct of a clouded Cane)
With earnest Eyes and round unthinking Face,
He first the Snuff-box open'd, then the Case,
And thus broke out – 'My Lord, why, what the Devil?
'Z—ds! damn the Lock! 'fore Gad, you must be civil!
'Plague on't! 'tis past a jest – nay prithee, Pox!
'Give her the Hair' – he spoke, and rapp'd his Box.
(123-130)

Brief though the description is, "earnest eyes and round unthinking face" we can see him instantly and his speech shows that Pope can do anything with the couplet – even incoherence.

After the bluster come the tears and Belinda bemoans her fate. She wishes she had never come to Hampton Court, that she had stayed at home and said her prayers. Anything rather than this disgrace, but the last of her list of 'anythings' is a couplet so cheekily ambiguous as to cast doubt on all that has gone before.

> Oh hadst thou, Cruel! been content to seize
> Hairs less in Sight, or any Hairs but these!
>
> (175-6)

At the beginning of the fifth and final Canto is a speech which Pope did not include until an edition of 1717. It is, however, one of the poem's major achievements. Back in 1709 Pope had published in Tottel's *Miscellanies* a translation of a speech by Sarpendon in *The Iliad*. In it the Trojans are facing defeat and Sarpendon urges them to stand firm and show fortitude in the face of death. Clarissa, in a speech which echoes that of Sarpendon at so many points, urges Belinda to accept that their lives are useless displays of vanity "Unless good Sense preserve what Beauty gains". Where Sarpendon had argued

> But since, alas, ignoble Age must come,
> Disease, and Death's inexorable Doom;
> The Life which others pay, let Us bestow,
> And give to Fame what we to Nature owe;
> Brave, tho' we fall; and honour'd if we live;
> Or let us Glory gain, or Glory give.

Clarissa insists that:

> But since, alas, frail Beauty must decay,
> Curl'd or uncurl'd, since Locks will turn to grey;
> Since painted, or not painted, all shall fade,
> And she who scorns a Man, must die a Maid;
> What then remains but well our Pow'r to use,
> And keep Good-humour still whate'er we lose?
>
> (25-30)

This is, it can be claimed, the central moral statement of the poem. A satire must have a firm moral basis if it is to be anything more than a burlesque or lampoon. But these lines are also a moving lament on the frailty of human existence and the transience of beauty.

Naturally, the other girls reject outright everything Clarissa has to say, dismissing her as a prude.

What ensues is chaos. They all begin to fight – sometimes with words which parody the clichés of popular love poems – Thalestris "scatters death around from both her eyes." But Belinda gets far more physical – throwing snuff into the Baron's face and threatening him with a bodkin – a bodkin with a comic history as complex as any epic hero's sword. But the Baron is not afraid.

> 'Boast not my Fall, (he cry'd), insulting Foe!
> Thou by some other shalt be laid as low.
> Nor think, to die dejects my lofty Mind:
> All that I dread is leaving you behind!'
>
> (97-101)

Empty words they sound, but once we recognise that 'to die' was an 18th-century colloquialism for an orgasm, and that to 'get laid' is still in common use, then the innuendos become all too clear again. There always has been sex in this Battle of the Sexes.

But the Goddess of Love, we now remember, had only granted the Baron half his prayer. He has 'obtain'd' the lock but now he has lost it; it cannot be found anywhere. Only the *Muse,* says Pope, saw it rise into the skies where it has become, seemingly, a comet. And so Pope is able to assure Belinda (and Arabella Fermor) of a lasting fame.

> When, after Millions slain, your self shall die;
> When those fair Suns shall set, as set they must,
> And all those Tresses shall be laid in Dust;
> This Lock, the Muse shall consecrate to Fame,
> And 'midst the Stars inscribe *Belinda's* Name!
>
> (146-150)

The poem was a great success. Except in the eyes of John Dennis. Humourless as ever, and ever hostile to Pope, he singled out the line "Hairs less in Sight, or any Hairs but these" insisting that while Pope *claimed* that Belinda had good breeding, modesty and virtue, he had "in Reality and in Fact made her an artificial Dawbing Jilt, a Tomrigg, a Virago and lady of the Lake." One has to grant him his own power with words.

But Johnson declared it "the most ingenious and the most delightful of all his compositions." And even Hazlitt, at a time when Pope's reputation had fallen almost out of sight, wrote that *The Rape of the Lock* was "the triumph of insignificance, the apotheosis of foppery and folly. It is the perfection of the mock-heroic!" And subsequent critics have agreed with him.

4

'Elegy to the Memory of an Unfortunate Lady' and *Eloisa to Abelard*

In his *Life of Pope* Johnson said of the 'Elegy to the Memory of an Unfortunate Lady' "... the tale is not skilfully told; it is not easy to discover the character of either the lady or her guardian." And he was right.

The poem opens rather melodramatically. The ghost of a young woman appears one moonlit night and beckons to the speaker to follow her into a nearby "glade". She is carrying a sword with which she has evidently killed herself. This immediately raises problems for us. Johnson defined *suicide* as "the horrid crime of destroying oneself." The Church regarded it as a mortal sin, and the law still held that suicides were to be buried in the public highway with a stake driven through them. So how could this Lady be described as 'Unfortunate', and how could she have deserved an 'Elegy'? One answer is that this poem, like the *Pastorals* and *Windsor-Forest*, is following a literary tradition – that of the Latin elegies of Ovid which celebrated, in lofty tones, some heroic or noble death. We are explicitly told that she played "a Roman's part" and the speaker asks whether it is a crime in heaven (as a ghost she is clearly not at rest there) to have loved too well.

> Is there no bright reversion in the sky,
> For those who greatly think, or bravely die?
> (9-11)

However, if these events had taken place in Rome, there would have *been* no problem about her being buried in holy ground. But later, the suggestion that insincere mourners might soon have been seen attending "midnight dances, and the publick show" sounds very much like 18th-century London. In truth, it is probably both and neither. The melodrama is far more suggestive of the Gothic and it is not surprising that the sentimental tone of this 'Elegy' made it one of the few pieces by Pope which were still admired in the early years of the 19th century. It had a Romantic appeal. It could be the synopsis of one of those Horror Novels which were popular at the time and which Jane Austen satirised so cleverly in *Northanger Abbey*.

Although the ghostly lady has beckoned the young man into the glade, she does not say a word to him. Indeed, as far as the narrative goes, she hardly needs to be there at all. He knows her story already and it is he who tells it to us. She committed suicide because her guardian had prevented her from marrying the love of her heart and the speaker calls down some splendidly stirring curses not only on him but on his entire family.

> Thus shall your wives, and thus your children fall;
> On all the line a sudden vengeance waits,
> And frequent hearses shall besiege your gates.
> There passengers shall stand, and pointing say,
> (While the long fun'rals blacken all the way)
> 'Lo these were they, whose souls the Furies steel'd,
> And curs'd with hearts unknowing how to yield.'
> (36-42)

To complete the tragedy she had even died alone in a foreign land.

> By foreign hands thy dying eyes were clos'd,
> By foreign hands thy decent limbs compos'd,
> (51-2)

But, unhallowed though the ground might have been, such was her sanctity that "The ground [is] now sacred by thy reliques made." A very ambiguous theological notion.

The poem ends with the speaker/poet foretelling his own death and sadly predicting that the memory of the 'Unfortunate Lady' will die with him, which makes us wonder whether it might have been he who was her lover.

Precise answers to such questions are hard to find in this poem, but as with Shakespeare's *Sonnets*, much useless energy has been spent on trying to discover who the various characters *really* were. Joseph Warton, who produced an edition of Pope's collected works at the end of the century, was convinced that it was a true story. "If this elegy be so excellent, it may be ascribed to this cause, that the occasion of it was real, for it is certainly an indisputable maxim that Nature is more powerful than fancy." Even so, for all his assertiveness, he could offer no plausible candidates. Johnson also tried and failed. "The lady's name and adventures I have sought with fruitless inquiry," he confessed. There were nevertheless plenty of theories. Some knew for certain that she was a woman of 'eminent rank and large fortune', while others were equally certain that she was 'ill-shaped and deformed'. At least six different ladies were *named*, including a Mrs Withinbury who, it was claimed, was in love with Pope himself and was prevented from marrying him by her guardian, who sent her to a nunnery where she hanged herself. Swords, presumably, were in rather short supply in nunneries at that time.

It is something of a hotchpotch of a poem, but it does have its good moments and it seems churlish not to credit Pope with enough imagination to have made it up.

The last word must however go to Samuel Johnson who clearly had no time for heroines of this type. "She seems to have been impertinent," he wrote, "violent and ungovernable." And adding finally, "Poetry has not often been worse employed than in dignifying the amorous fury of a raving girl."

For all its uncertainties (I would not go so far as to call them failures) the 'Elegy' does rise to a new challenge. As we have already seen, the balance inherent in the structure of the couplet makes it the ideal medium for reasoning, for intellectual argument, the weighing of opposites and the logical sequencing of ideas, but in the 'Elegy' he successfully used it to give voice to emotion. The emotion, it could be argued, is rather shallow, is not really explored or developed, and is that of an accepted literary genre, but then in *Eloisa to Abelard*, a poem written at about the same time, he goes several steps further; the emotions being far more complex and expressed with a striking dramatic intensity. It proved, not surprisingly, to be one of Pope's most popular poems and even in the Romantic Period, when his stock had fallen very low indeed, one critic went so far as to say that, "Nothing of the kind has ever been produced equal to it for pathos, painting and melody."

Spoken in the first person and in the voice of a woman, it occupies a unique position in Pope's oeuvre, yet there is one important respect in which it is of a piece with all the rest as it too depends on a recognised literary tradition: that of the Heroic Epistles, the *Heroides*, of Ovid: letters written by famous women to their absent lovers.

This time Pope did not have to concern himself with narrating the tale; it was already well known. Peter Abelard was a French intellectual, a philosopher and theologian, a brilliant scholar, a teacher with such charisma that he was one of the most famous men of his day – in modern terms he was a *celebrity*. Among the students who crowded into his lectures was Eloisa, a young girl of outstanding academic ability and great beauty. Her uncle engaged Abelard to give her individual tuition and invited him to move into their house. Eloisa was 18 and he was 40, but very soon, as he put it himself, "There was more kissing than teaching; my hands found themselves at her breasts more often than on the book."

Inevitably she became pregnant. They married secretly, as if the fact had become known it would have meant an end to his future in the Church and so the end to his academic career too. When openly challenged, Eloisa, who had been against their marriage in the first place, denied it, hoping that her denial would help Abelard, but her uncle was so enraged at this treatment of his niece that he hired two thugs to break into Abelard's rooms one night and castrate him. Abelard then became a monk and Eloisa a nun. Years later, when one of Abelard's friends was seemingly experiencing problems in his love life, Abelard wrote to him telling him his own story and the letter fell (as these things do) into the hands of Eloisa, re-awakening her memories and her passion. This then began a famous correspondence between them which was ultimately translated into English in 1713 and it was this which inspired Pope. In his Preface he writes that they are letters which "give so lively a picture of the struggles of grace and nature, virtue and passion", a parallelism which, I think, gives an indication of the way in which he saw the couplet being admirably suited to express Eloisa's situation.

The opening of the poem is every bit as Gothic as that of the 'Elegy', with personifications of *Contemplation* and *Melancholy* reminiscent of Milton's *Il Penseroso*, but in this case the Gothic element is more than simply atmospheric; it mirrors Eloisa's feelings, with images of the "deep solitude" of the cloister and the "darksom" walls which enclose her. She has not though, as she insists, become as cold as the stone.

> Tho' cold like you, unmov'd, and silent grown
> I have not yet forgot my self to stone.

>> (23-4)

She still has a "rebel nature" (26), admits that her heart is guilty of a "close disguise" (11) and in a line which sounds almost blasphemous asserts that Abelard is far from forgotten, "All is not Heav'n's while Abelard has part". (25)

She strives to suppress her feelings, but cannot. She has hold of his letter and she kisses his name; she struggles not to write it but has done so already. Her struggle is enacted in the antithetical couplets

Oh name for ever sad! for ever dear!
Still breath'd in sighs, still usher'd with a tear
(31-2)

and in the contrasting rhymes such as *restrain/in vain.* (27-8)

She begs him to write to her so that they may share in each other's grief and then she begins to recount their story. She does so as this is *not* in fact a letter. It is a meditation, her thoughts prior to writing a letter, and, being a poem, these thoughts are directed towards us as readers. We can see that she idolised Abelard, but she was no 'wronged maid'. She wanted him. "Nor wish'd an Angel whom I lov'd a man." (70) Hers was a forceful and passionate nature. She had rejected marriage, she reminds him, so as to preserve his career, but she also glories in the freedom of being his *mistress.*

If there be yet another name more free,
More fond than mistress, make me that to thee!
(89-90)

One of the strengths of this poem is its sudden and passionate changes in mood and direction. From recalling the bliss of their love, her mind is all of a sudden flooded by the memory of the assault on him and his castration. Even so, it is his physical presence she wants and she says so in lines of quite explicit sexuality.

Still on that breast enamour'd let me lie,
Still drink delicious poison from thy eye,
Pant on thy lip, and to thy heart be prest;
Give all thou canst – and let me dream the rest.
(121-4)

A moment later, however, and she is determined to "quit Abelard for God" (128), but it is these seeming inconsistencies which give her a coherent identity and make her all the more convincing as a dramatic creation, for the poem strikes me as far more of a dramatic monologue than an epistle. It is, of course, a drama not of action but of feelings, the feelings of a woman trapped inside a convent, but alive in her memory and in her imagination, but trapped too – and this is her tragic dilemma – between those classic and irreconcilable claims: duty and desire. And again Pope uses the balance of the couplet to enact the dilemma.

> I ought to grieve, but cannot what I ought;
> I mourn the lover, not lament the fault;
> I view my crime, but kindle at the view,
> Repent old pleasures, and sollicit new.
>
> (183-6)

When she does try to turn to God, comparing the serenity of the religious life, " The world forgetting, by the world forgot", (208) with the destructive passion of her dreams, the language is again explicit, as in her dreams it is clear that he has not been castrated, "Fancy restores what vengeance snatch'd away" (226) and when she paints a picture of herself at mass, with her mind very much elsewhere, even a reference to "swelling organ" seems ambiguous. At one moment she is ready to dare damnation for Abelard, the next she bids him to "fly me, fly me!" There is no attempt on her part, or on Pope's, to reconcile these conflicting claims. He is not concerned with her salvation or her damnation but with her life as it is being lived at that moment. We are witness to what has been called "the humanising power of tragic passion". She *endures*. And I am reminded of some lines from Wordsworth's poem *Michael*.

> There is a comfort in the strength of love;
> 'Twill make a thing endurable which else
> Would break the heart.

It would be possible to condemn Eloisa for her laxity but Pope never does. He invites our compassion and our understanding.

In the closing moments of the poem she envisages her death and wants Abelard to be there to grant her the last rites, but even here the language has a physicality to it. He is to, "Suck my last breath, and catch my flying soul!" (324) Her hope that they might be re-united in death was granted as they were buried side by side in the Monastery of the Paraclete.

In conclusion Pope puts into her mind the image of some "future bard" who so shares her grief and emotion that he may be able to tell her story. "He best can paint 'em, who shall feel 'em most." (366)

And there is a parallel, as Pope's physical disability can be seen as having trapped him and deprived him of a satisfactory and contented sex life, but this poem clearly shows us that his emotions were in no way disabled. And in a letter to Martha Blount, one of his Roman Catholic neighbours in Berkshire, he writes that "The Epistle to Eloise grows warm, and begins to have some Breathings of the Heart in it, which may make posterity think I was in love." And he may well have been in love with her. His relationship with her was one of his most important and long-lasting. Gossip claimed that she was his mistress and even that they were secretly married. What is certain is that she was the chief beneficiary in his will.

When the poem was published he also wrote to Lady Mary Wortley Montagu enclosing his *Workes* and saying that in the Epistle, " ... you will find one passage, that I can't tell whether to wish you should understand, or not." Lady Mary has been described as " ... vivacious, ambitious, aggressive, self-educated far beyond the attainments of most women of her time, and beautiful." At the time of the letter, she was in Constantinople where her husband was British Envoy to the Sultanate and so the passage might well have been

> Condemn'd whole years in absence to deplore,
> And image charms he must behold no more,
> (361-2)

Pope was to write in a poem *To Mr Gay* that "Joy ... only dwells where WORTLEY casts her eyes." If it was ever a serious passion, it was always to be a hopeless one, and in later years it turned, as we shall see, into something of a very different nature.

The *Workes* to which he refers in the letter was a volume published in 1717 including everything that he had written up to that time. It has been described as "a handsome book, issued in sumptuous quarto, folio, and large folio formats, printed on several qualities of paper, and embellished with engraved headpieces, tailpieces and pictorial initials." It has also been described as "a monument to vanity". He was still under thirty; his future as a poet looked assured, and yet in the next decade he did not publish another original poem of any significance.

5

Homer, a Landscape Garden and Shakespeare

In any league table of literary types and genres, the epic has always and without question occupied first place, and I think it can safely be said that it had always been Pope's ambition to write one. He told Joseph Spence that when he was little more than twelve years old he had begun to write the story of Alcander, Prince of Rhodes. "I wrote four books toward it," he told him, "of about a thousand verses each" and he was sufficiently enamoured of it to have kept it by him until 1723, when he was 35, and his friend the Bishop of Rochester suggested, probably wisely, that he should burn it. But his life-long love affair with the epic had begun even earlier than that. At the age of eight he had discovered John Ogilby's translation of Homer in a "great edition with pictures" and it was from that, he told Spence, that he had "caught the itch of poetry". And setting out on his professional career by writing pastorals, as had the great epic poets Virgil and Milton before him, would seem to indicate that he knew the correct course of apprenticeship such an ambition was expected to take. As we saw, when considering *The Rape of the Lock*, 18th-century English society was not conducive to epic, but the 'itch' could to some extent be satisfied by translation. Pope had already published some extracts from Homer in Tonson's *Miscellany* and in 1713 he declared his intention to translate *The Iliad* in its entirety. It is a poem which totals some sixteen thousand lines and it was to take him six years to complete, years during which he could not be expected to write anything of his own. On another occasion he told Spence, "I should certainly have written an Epic Poem, if I had not engaged in the translation of Homer."

Not everyone thought the translation was a good idea. Robert Harley urged him against it. "So good a writer ought not to be a translator," he argued. And there were times when Pope himself was not sure he was doing the right thing. "What terrible moments does one feel after one has engaged for a large work!" he said. "In the beginning of my translating *The Iliad*, I wished anybody would hang me, a hundred times. It sat so heavily on my mind at first." His mind might sometimes have given him doubts, but there was a passion which was an unstoppable driving force, a passion for Homer's powers of *Invention*, a passion which is evident throughout his *Introduction*. He wrote, "It is to the strength of this amazing Invention we are to attribute that unequalled fire and rapture, which is so forcible in Homer, that no man of true poetical spirit is master of himself while he reads him."

But Pope was sufficiently master of himself to recognise that the publishing deal which he had negotiated with Bernard Lintot for a sumptuous subscription edition would earn him enough to guarantee him financial security and independence for the rest of his life. It is never easy to equate 18th-century financial values with those of today, but were we to say that it brought him the equivalent of half a million pounds we would not be far wrong.

As well as being a financial success, Pope's translation was also an outstanding critical success. Dr Johnson called it, "the noblest version of poetry which the world has ever seen", and in our own day the not-easily-pleased critic George Steiner insisted that it is "a masterpiece in its own right and an epic which, so far as English goes, comes second only to Milton." Of course nothing is universally popular, but when Richard Bentley, the most distinguished classical scholar of the time, made his famous remark, "It is a pretty poem, Mr Pope, but you must not call it Homer", he was stating what ought to have been obvious. It is not Homer. It is Alexander Pope's version of Homer. He himself called it "something parallel, tho' not the same." It was intended for the readers of Pope's own day, readers who, though there was vulgarity enough in their own lives as Hogarth has shown us, nevertheless shuddered at any vulgarity in the epic and who placed a far higher premium on literary decorum than did Homer's audience. To cite one example. In Book 11 of *The Iliad* Ajax has been fighting like a lion, but when forced to retreat does so reluctantly, stubbornly, like, as Homer puts it, an ass. In Samuel Butler's translation we read "like some lazy ass that has had many a cudgel broken about his back". Now in his notes Pope makes it clear that he greatly admires the contrast. "The character of a stubborn but undaunted warrior is perfectly maintained, and must strike the reader at the first view." But *ass* is a 'vile' word and he cannot bring himself to use it when referring to a great military hero. He explains that " … a translator owes so much to the taste of the age in which he lives, as not to make too great a compliment to the former; and this induced me to omit the mention of the word ass in the translation." But his alternative, "As the slow beast with heavy strength endu'd" has a genuinely cumbersome sound to it which is far superior to Richmond Lattimore's "As when a donkey, stubborn and hard to move, goes into a cornfield."

That terse quality which is the mark of Pope's couplets may not seem to be best suited to narrative, but there are moments when it achieves what other translations fail to do and that is to produce memorable lines. Towards the end of the work, when Achilles is consoling Priam, Samuel Butler has him saying, "We will hide our sorrows in our hearts, for weeping will not avail us." And Lattimore, ostensibly in verse, gives us, "There is not any advantage to be won from grim lamentation." Pope does it in nine succinct words. "To mourn, avails not: Man is born to bear." And we realise that this translation is the work, not of a translator, but of a major poet. That is the difference.

Beginning in 1715 the volumes appeared one a year until the sixth and last was produced in 1720. One would have thought that six years of translating would have been enough, but no. Almost immediately he began work on *The Odyssey*. This time, however, he employed two assistants: Elijah Fenton, who translated four books, and William Broome, who certainly worked on eight, some say 12. One contemporary wit suggested that it was *Broome* who swept the way for Pope to follow, but Pope did not simply accept all that his assistants had written; he re-worked their versions assiduously. Later he was even reluctant to admit how much they had done and it is said that he didn't pay them very well either.

This collaboration might be one of the reasons why there seems to be some spark lacking in Pope's *Odyssey*. It has been called a *reflection* rather than a re-creation of the original. But they are two very different poems; quite possibly written by two very different poets. *The Iliad* is, one could say, a true epic, expressly concerned with the fate of nations, with warfare and the deeds of kings, generals and heroes. *The Odyssey*, in contrast, and especially in the latter half when Odysseus has arrived back home on Ithaca, features a crowd of totally disreputable 'suitors' indulging in a good deal of highly un-heroic, not to say drunkenly yobbish behaviour. It also gives prominent rôles to members of the lower orders: to servants, swineherds, even to beggars. In Book 18, for instance, Iris, the resident beggar in the palace, is about to fight with Odysseus, but then tries to back out. Antinous, one of the suitors, threatens that if he loses

> Instant thou sail'st, to Echetus resign'd;
> A tyrant, fiercest of the tyrant kind,
> Who casts thy mangled ears and nose a prey
> To hungry dogs, and lops the man away.

Those final words are something of a smoke-screen as we can see from the lively brutality of a recent version.

> Well, I tell you this straight: if he wins, you're going
>   on the next black ship to King Echetos,
> And you know what he'll do, don't you? Skin you alive
>   he will; cut off your nose and your ears;
> and rip your bollocks off and feed them to his dogs!

We can hardly expect Pope to have used language such as that, but in his *Postscript* to *The Odyssey* he did face up to the problem and claimed that "There is real beauty in an easy, pure, perspicuous description even of a low action." And he went on, "The question is, how far a Poet, in pursuing the description or image of an action, can attach himself to little circumstances, without vulgarity or trifling? What particulars are proper, and enliven the image; or what are impertinent and clog it?"

A notorious example of a clog comes in Book 21 when one of the suitors (as the same recent version puts it)

> ... picked up a cow's hoof and flung it
> at Odysseus.

Cow's hoof is too much for Pope. Not in an epic.

> ... and of the steer before him placed,
> That sinewy fragment at Ulysses cast,
> Where to the pastern-bone, by nerves combin'd.
> The well-horned foot indissolubly join'd.

As one of Pope's 19th-century editors said of these lines. "I fear we must agree with the censure pronounced by Mr. W. on this circumlocutory and exaggerated style in describing such an incident as that of throwing an ox-hoof." Blind to any faults in his own style apparently.

If, as has been suggested, Pope was less enthusiastic about *The Odyssey*, the question is why he chose to do it. One answer may be that, despite the advance he had had for *The Iliad*, he needed the money as his way of living, together with his cost of living, had changed greatly. In 1719 he had moved from London to the Thames-side village of Twickenham, which had become very fashionable among artists, writers and musicians. It was a modest enough dwelling Pope moved into, but he quickly set about turning it into a 'Palladian' villa, and, what's more, a villa with a *garden*; a garden which was to have an influence on 18th-century taste and fashion perhaps more far-reaching even than his poetry, as he was to become, as a leading authority on the subject has called him, "the founder of English landscape gardening."

That gardening was very much to the forefront of his thinking while he was working on *The Iliad* can be seen from the imagery he used in the second paragraph of his *Preface*. "Our author's work is a wild paradise, where, if we cannot see all the beauties so distinctly as in an ordered garden, it is only because the number of them is infinitely greater. It is like a copious nursery, which contains the seeds and first productions of every kind, out of which those who followed him have but selected some particular plants, each according to his fancy, to cultivate and beautify."

Very briefly, the history of landscape gardening at that time is that in 1660 the return of Charles II from exile in France brought with it a fashion for all things French and this included the type of formal garden seen at Versailles and Fontainebleau: that rather soulless, geometric regularity – the straight lines, the vast gravel terraces with their tightly-clipped box hedges and this prevailed for well over half a century. But in 1713 Pope opened a decisive attack on it in an essay in *The Guardian*. He particularly opposed and mocked the fad for topiary, where people were "better pleased to have our Trees in the most awkward Figures of Man and Animals than in the most regular of their own." His overall argument is best summed up when he says, "There is certainly something in the amiable Simplicity of unadorned Nature, that spreads over the Mind a more noble sort of Tranquillity, and a loftier Sensation of Pleasure, than can be raised from the nicer Scenes of Art" (*nicer* here means something like finicky). It is interesting in this context to think back to lines 68-9 of *An Essay on Criticism*:

> First follow NATURE, and your Judgment frame
> By her just Standard, which is still the same:

lines which point to the overall cohesion of Pope's thinking as poet, artist and gardener.

Pope's essay in *The Guardian* was one of the first steps in a movement which resulted in the creation of gardens which looked as much like nature as possible, where hard lines were softened, where trees were planted in groves instead of avenues of straight lines and where lakes with tranquil expanses of water replaced ornate fountains. It was the movement which gave us the great landscape gardens of Stourhead and Stowe. Of course, in comparison with these great estates, Pope's five acres were miniscule, so miniscule in fact that Lord Bathurst threatened that if Pope failed to pay him a visit at Cirencester Park he would send one of his "wood-carts and bring away your whole house and gardens, and stick it in the middle of Oakley-wood, where it will never be heard of any more, unless some of the children find it in Nutting season and take possession of it thinking I have made it for them."

I think the tone of this tells us a great deal about the friendship between the two men, but Bathurst was not Pope's only wealthy and aristocratic gardening friend. Others included Robert Dormer of Rousham House in Oxfordshire, Lord Cobham who built Stowe, and most important of all, Lord Burlington of Chiswick House, who introduced Pope to William Kent, the garden designer who said that "all gardening is landscape painting" and of whom Horace Walpole said, "Mahomet imagined an Elysium; Kent created many." These men created magnificent gardens on a grand scale, but it was the diminutive Pope in his five acres they went to for ideas, guidance and advice.

Five acres may not have seemed much, but Pope could have taken some consolation from the famous description of Alcinous' garden in Book 7 of *The Odyssey*, which, in his own translation, reads:

45

> Close to the Gates a spacious Garden lies,
> From Storms defended, and inclement Skies:
> Four Acres was th'allotted Space of Ground,
> Fenc'd with a green Enclosure all around.
> Tall thriving Trees confest the fruitful Mold;
> The red'ning Apple ripens here to Gold,
> Here the blue Figg with luscious Juice o'erflows,
> With deeper Red the full Pomegranate glows,
> The Branch here bends beneath the weighty Pear,
> And verdant Olives flourish round the Year.

Comparatively small though it may have been, Pope's garden was as compact and as complex as any of his couplets. From the plan which John Serle, his gardener, drew up we can see that it had a bowling green, a vineyard, several small lawns, an orangery and a kitchen garden. There was a mound from which his visitors could view the river, a shell temple and an obelisk in memory of his mother. Altogether it was as carefully planned and wrought as was his poetry. The two main occupations of his life reflect each other, and this is equally true of the garden's most famous feature: *Pope's Grotto.*

A main road from Hampton to Richmond passed outside his house, dividing it from the garden, and so he obtained permission to dig a tunnel under the house. Johnson was rather sarcastic about it, saying that he had "extracted an ornament from an inconvenience, and vanity provided a grotto where necessity enforced a passage." Ornamental it certainly was, with ores and minerals embedded in its walls, pieces of marble and crystal, reflecting mirrors, lava from Vesuvius and even gold ore from Peru. It was a feature he worked on as he worked on his poems, changing and adding continually. He was a perfectionist.

Clearly the Grotto meant more to him than simply a convenient way of getting from one part of his property to another and just what it meant can perhaps again be gauged from some lines in *The Odyssey*:

> Descending Vines the shelving cavern screen,
> With purple Clusters blushing through the Green,
> Four limpid Fountains from the Clefts distil;
> And ev'ry Fountain pours a several Rill,
> In mazy Windings wandering down the Hill;

Where bloomy Meads with vivid Greens were crown'd,
And glowing Violets threw Odours round,
A Scene where, if a God should cast his Sight,
A God might gaze and wander with Delight.

What had delighted Pope most during the initial excavations for his grotto was the discovery of a spring of pure water. The Muses were always associated with springs and vice versa. And when Joseph Spence brought him a stone from the Grotto of Egaria in Rome – though not herself a muse, Egaria, a bringer of wisdom and philosophy, was often linked with them – then for Pope the belief that it was now a cave of inspiration, a place where he could communicate with his Muse, must have seemed complete. In a drawing of the Grotto by Kent we see Pope seated in the centre and writing. It was the ideal retreat – a writer's dream.

But it became so famous that he was plagued by visitors wanting to see it. At the beginning of his *Epistle to Dr Arbuthnot* he complains:

What Walls can guard me, or what Shades can hide?
They pierce my Thickets, thro' my Grot they glide.

After his death it became something of a tourist attraction, so much so that in 1807 Baroness Howe, its then occupant, felt so "inconvenienced" by them that she had the whole building pulled down! The Grotto is still there, beneath the buildings of a school, but only a few fragments of its decoration remain.

By 1721, two years after moving to Twickenham, the influence of the muses was not yet strong enough to bring him back to poetry. As he explained in a letter to John Caryll, "I am become, by due gradation of dullness, from a poet to a translator, and from a translator, a mere editor."

It was Jacob Tonson, the nephew of the more famous publisher of Pope's earliest work, who had commissioned him to edit the collected plays of Shakespeare. Why Pope agreed to this is a puzzle. The financial incentive does not seem to have been great and he must have been aware of just what an onerous task he was undertaking. No one had, as yet, fully co-ordinated the bewildering array of quartos and it would have needed a man of great patience, interested in linguistic minutiae, and with a real knowledge of Elizabethan language and grammar. Pope was not that man. One of the interesting things about his edition is the result of Augustan *decorum*. Passages and expressions which he thought would demean Shakespeare, passages which he thought Shakespeare could not possibly have written (such as the Porter's soliloquy in *Macbeth*) are relegated to the foot of the page and contain a total of over fifteen hundred lines. Maynard Mack, a generous biographer, says that Pope "botched the job badly." But ironically the *botch* was the stimulus for his next real poem.

His Edition – all six volumes of it – came out in 1725 and the following year there was published a two hundred page quarto with the grandiloquent title of "*SHAKESPEARE* restored: Or, A SPECIMEN of the Many ERRORS, As Well *Committed*, as *Unamended*, by Mr. POPE In his Late EDITION of this POET. DESIGNED Not only to correct the said EDITION, but to restore the True READING of SHAKESPEARE in all the *Editions* ever yet publish'd." It was the work of Lewis Theobald, a man as strange as this title would suggest. Much of the work is as Maynard Mack puts it, "so much nonsense, so many tiresome displays of irrelevant learning, self-gratulations", but not all of it; he did know his Elizabethan drama, and even apart from the title, there was enough sound criticism of Pope's errors, together with some personal slurs, to have angered him greatly.

For some time Pope had been thinking of writing a work in which he could give vent to his feelings about what he saw as the miserable state of contemporary literature and Theobald became the leading figure in just such a poem, *The Dunciad*, which made its first appearance in 1728, but went through so many variations, changes and different editions – the last in 1743, the year before Pope's death – that it seems wiser to consider it fully in a later chapter.

6

Essay on Man

Having spent more than a decade translating Homer and editing Shakespeare, Pope must have realised that to re-establish his reputation as a poet he would need to publish a work of some substance and what he settled on, the "opus magnum", as he called it in a letter to Swift, was to be a poem, or rather a sequence of poems, which would propose a "system of ethics in the Horatian way", by which he meant a series of epistles or verse letters. The themes he saw it covering were as serious and as diverse as: the Nature of Man, the limits of Human Reason, Civil and Ecclesiastical Polity, and the Use of Education, Learning and Riches. It is an intimidating list and while we can see that some of these topics do feature later, in a rather more light-hearted manner, in the *Moral Essays*, the scheme as a whole never came to completion. Only his views on Man and Human Reason ever achieved a final form in his poem *An Essay on Man*, which he sub-titled *The First Book of Ethic Principles*.

An interesting parallel can be made here with Wordsworth, who, urged on by Coleridge, also planned a long philosophical poem, but only completed what came to be known as *The Prelude*. Wordsworth's poem has as its sub-title *The Growth of a Poet's Mind*, meaning his own mind, and it is totally autobiographical. It begins with his childhood and tells us stories about him stealing a boat, skating with his school friends on the ice at night and so on. Now no 18th-century poet would ever have written about such trivial, childish things. Children in those days were dressed as young adults and treated simply as incomplete specimens of the species waiting to grow up, and until they did so they were of no real importance. There was no such thing, for example, during the first half of the century, as children's literature. It was as if childhood had not yet been invented and that is equally true of autobiography; the word did not even appear in the language until Southey coined it in 1809.

But there was an audience for poetry in Pope's day. As James Sutherland put it, "The poet was a member of polite society addressing himself to his equals, and though poetry was a special mode of communication it did not exempt him from the normal usages of polite society." If reading poetry was a social activity, then the writing of it was a 'social art' abiding by clear social conventions. And it is still true today that in any social gathering we do not, unless we are total bores, talk incessantly about ourselves. It was not done in 18th-century society and it was not done in their literature.

Society also regarded with great suspicion anything which appeared excessively personal, individual or 'original'. The OED does not record the word *originality* as meaning something 'different from anything that has appeared before' until 1787. Prior to that an 'original' was *an eccentric*, or *a buffoon*.

What we have to remember is that it was excessive individuality in matters of politics, but especially in religion, which had led to the horrors of a civil war which was still fresh in people's minds. No one wanted a return to that. In addition, in the field of poetry there was a natural reaction against what had been popular in the previous generation and that included the irregularities and oddities of the metaphysical poets of the 17th century. (To understand this one needs to think of Crashaw and Cowley rather than of Donne and Herbert.) To be *fanciful* was not fashionable. As Thomas Rhymer put it so memorably, "A poet is not to leave his reason, and blindly abandon himself to follow fancy, for then his fancy might be monstrous, might be singular, and please nobody's maggot but his own."

The 18th century was also becoming increasingly interested in science, and was tending to favour those kinds of truth which are universal and demonstrable. General truths: "What oft was thought, but ne'er so well express'd". Hence in his poems Pope writes about Man in general, and not about himself as an individual.

To re-establish his reputation was not going to be easy. His *Dunciad* of 1728 had openly attacked several people making him a new set of enemies who would be eager to get their revenge. His *Epistle to Burlington* (which will be looked at in the next chapter) published in 1731, had been savaged, but *An Essay on Man* was unlike anything he had ever written, so, using a bookseller who had not published him before, he issued the first *Epistle* anonymously in 1733. The ploy worked. The poem was showered with praise, much of it coming from writers who had been openly hostile to him, and there was no way, to their great grief, that they could go back on their word once his authorship was known.

In Pope's prefatory *Design* to the poem he explained that his aim was to present "a temperate yet not inconsistent, and a short yet not imperfect system of Ethics", but that it was to be seen only as a preliminary, as he put it, "opening the fountains". There would be more to follow in which he would "deduce the rivers, to follow them in their course". Interestingly, he says that he might have written it in prose, but chose verse, "even rhyme", because "principles, maxims, or precepts so written both strike the reader more strongly at first, and are more easily retained by him afterwards."

The poem opens in the relaxed 'Horatian way'; so very relaxed in fact that the friend Pope is addressing, St. John Bolingbroke, appears to be asleep. "Awake, my St. John!" it begins and in the opening lines it seems that we are about to listen in to a conversation between these two 18th-century gentlemen as they stroll through the grounds of their estate, but Bolingbroke soon disappears and does not come back into the poem until the very end, and the conversational tone which Pope was later to perfect in his *Epistles* and *Satires*, is abandoned too. Before long we are not only being spoken *to* but *at*; even at times, it has to be said, harangued.

This was to be a didactic poem, and its aim, we are told, would be to "vindicate the ways of God to Man." Now this is clearly an echo – more than an echo – of Milton's assertion at the outset of *Paradise Lost* that he intends to "justify the ways of God to men." It is the change of verbs which attracts us at first, but even a careful perusal of the OED suggests no real difference between them, using 'to justify' as part of the definition of 'vindicate'. But the significant change may be in the ending of the line, where *to men* becomes *to Man*. Milton's intention, I would suggest, is to explain to us, to men, God's actions, whereas Pope means to explain God's *attitude* towards us, not as individuals, but as a species, as Man, with a capital M. And as we soon see, God's attitude has not always looked friendly. Why is there evil? Why are there disasters? It is that which needs explanation, indeed *vindication*.

The *Essay* can be seen as being in part a refutation of the Roman poet Lucretius who, in his poem *de Rerum Natura* argued that the world had come about as a result of an accidental collision of atoms – an astonishing theory for a man writing in the first century BCE – and in contrast Pope asserts as early as line 6 that the universe might look like a "mighty maze" but is "not without a plan". He rejects such abstract theorising, insisting that we can only reason from what we know at first hand, yet at the same time he takes it for granted that the *Great Chain of Being* is not itself a theory but a fact and that we must accept that the position on it which God has given us in "his wisdom infinite" must be for the best. There are inevitably gradations in the chain, so it must be accepted that there are inequalities and limitations, so we should not bemoan our fate for we might indeed have been worse off:

> Then say not man's imperfect, Heav'n in fault;
> Say, rather Man's as perfect as he ought.
>
> (69-70)

Man differs significantly from the beasts below him on the chain in that he knows the future which awaits him, and that is death, but in recompense God has given to all mankind the gift of Hope – hope in the happiness of eternity.

If we complain about our position on the Great Chain, and would be higher, then it is pride which drives us, the same Sin of Pride which drove Satan to rebel. And it is pride which makes us regard ourselves as the most important thing in the universe; that the universe was created *for* us, a belief which leads us to consider those natural disasters which sometimes ruin our lives as being a failing on God's part. He could, we believe, have prevented them. However, we are, as Pope says, only a part of the general scheme of things; God acts "not by partial but by general laws" and so we are not in a position to comprehend the overall scheme. "'Tis but a part we see, and not a whole."

Suppose we were to be granted our wishes and suddenly found ourselves possessing finer senses – touch or smell for example – the result might be agonising:

> Or touch, if trembling alive all o'er,
> To smart and agonize at ev'ry pore?
> Or quick effluvia darting through the brain,
> Die of a rose in aromatic pain?
>
> (197-200)

There is a universal order and gradation in the Chain, we are told, and while we may seem, from our partial point of view, to be lacking in some respect compared with other creatures, we have Reason which more than compensates, and we should be content with that, as any break in the chain would lead not only to discord but to chaos.

Moving towards the close of the First Epistle, Pope states the argument succinctly in one couplet:

> All are but parts of one stupendous whole,
> Whose body, Nature is, and God the soul.
>
> (267-8)

And he concludes with a resounding declaration:

> All Nature is but Art, unknown to thee;
> All Chance, Direction, which thou canst not see;
> All Discord, Harmony, not understood;
> All partial Evil, universal Good;
> And, spite of Pride, in erring Reason's spite,
> One Truth is clear, 'Whatever IS, is RIGHT.'
>
> (289-94)

Taken in isolation, those last four words look very dubious and Voltaire satirised such blind optimism, as it appears, in *Candide*, where Dr. Pangloss is subjected to a whole series of disasters, while still proclaiming that ours is the best of all possible worlds, but this is to miss the essential point that while it may not be 'best' for the individual, it may be best for the system as a whole. Inequality is a necessary feature. Perfection would of necessity be unchanging, or it could not be perfection, but unchanging equality would be insupportable, would be tedious beyond belief, a state of things which Wallace Stevens recognised in his poem *Sunday Morning*:

> Is there no change of death in paradise?
> Does ripe fruit never fall? Or do the boughs
> Hang always heavy in that perfect sky,
> Unchanging, yet so like our perishing earth

Paradoxical though it seems, it may be, as Stevens suggests, that "Death is the mother of beauty".

After dealing with man and his relation to the universe, Epistle II is about Man as an individual, and it begins with the couplet:

> Know then thyself, presume not God to scan;
> The proper study of Mankind is Man.

The second line of which combines precision of thought with such economy of expression that it has become more than simply memorable, more than a 'quotation'; it has taken to itself the status of a proverb.

Again, we notice, he uses that word *Man*. Pope is by no means advocating self-analysis. It would be left to Wordsworth to cultivate the "egotistical sublime". Man, in Pope's view, not only occupies a midway point in the Great Chain of Being, but is also balanced between other contrasting states of being, and again it is the couplet which enables him to express this idea in some of the poem's most brilliant lines.

> Plac'd on this isthmus of a middle state,
> A being darkly wise, and rudely great;
> With too much knowledge for the Sceptic's side,
> With too much weakness for the Stoic's pride.
> (3-6)

> Still by himself abus'd, or disabus'd ;
> Created half to rise, and half to fall;
> Great Lord of all things, yet a prey to all;
> Sole judge of Truth, in endless Error hurl'd:
> The glory, jest, and riddle of the world!
> (14-8)

The choice of that word *isthmus* strikes me as so ingenious and so very apt.

Man has been blessed with Reason, but in the scale of things it is seen to be a very limited faculty. Pope looks at some of the great scientific achievements of the 18th century, but is dismissive of them. Even Newton, whom he genuinely admired, is, to the angelic powers, he says, as the rest of us are to apes, and while he might have been able to explain the workings of the universe, he could not "Describe or fix one movement of his Mind."

In the lines which follow there are some serious illogicalities. First we are told that, "What Reason weaves, by Passion is undone", but then ten lines later that:

> Two Principles in human nature reign;
> Self-love to urge, and Reason, to restrain.
>
> (53-4)

Is Reason a driving or a restraining force? But then we are told that they have the same objective:

> Self-love and Reason to one end aspire,
> Pain their aversion, Pleasure their desire.
>
> (87-8)

Next that we can do nothing unless we have both:

> On life's vast ocean diversely we sail,
> Reason the card, but Passion is the gale.
>
> (107-8)

Pope goes on to argue that we each have one Ruling Passion, which might overbalance us psychologically, were it not that Reason, this time a 'rectifier', steps in to bring about good from ill, producing *zeal* and *fortitude* from *anger*, *prudence* from *avarice*, and, mysteriously, *philosophy* from *sloth*. Nature, he claims, supplies us with the corresponding virtue nearest to our vice. Even Heaven steps in and "counter-works each folly and caprice", and disappoints the "effect of every vice". And as if this supremely optimistic view of human nature were not astonishing enough, we are then assured that no one "will change his neighbour with himself". Apparently we are all happy exactly as we are, the rich, the poor, the blind and the cripple. Does that include, we can feel ourselves asking, people who are only four foot six inches tall, are hunchbacked and who will later refer to this "long disease my life"?

The Epistle ends with a truly disparaging view of man. As we go through life, we are just playing with our toys, it seems. The toys may differ as we grow older – in middle age we want titles and fame; in old age our prayer books – but whatever, they are simply toys we play with until "life's poor play is o'er". And the final couplet is:

> See! and confess, one comfort still must rise,
> 'Tis this, Tho' Man's a fool, yet GOD IS WISE.
>
> (292-4)

At the outset we were "the glory, jest and riddle of the world!", but somewhere along the way we seem to have been robbed of our glory.

Epistle III begins with a reminder that "The Universal Cause Acts to one end, but acts by various laws" and having looked at man as an Individual Pope now goes on to a consideration of his relation to Society, setting out to show that the whole universe is one coherent social system – " a Chain of Love". (7)

We sometimes tend to think in our arrogance that it was all made for us, and us alone, but Pope argues that "Nothing is made wholly for itself, nor yet wholly for another." In an amusing but provocative image he says:

> See dying vegetables life sustain,
> See life dissolving vegetate again;
> All forms that perish other forms supply,
> (By turns we catch the vital breath, and die.)
> (15-8)

Man is somewhat different though, and in an astonishingly idealistic paragraph he suggests that we care for all the other animals:

> Man cares for all: to birds he gives his woods,
> To beasts his pastures, and to fish his floods;
> (57-8)

Of course man is going to eat all these animals after he has so kindly 'cared' for them, but God has ensured that they never guess what's coming to them. Man knows he is going to die, but God has eased the fear of it by giving him hope of an after-life, but we try not to think about it. Had Wordsworth been writing this, I think he might at this point have included that supremely honest line from Book V of *The Prelude*: "My drift, I fear, is scarcely obvious". In the second section Pope asserts, rather controversially I would have thought, that Reason is inferior to Instinct. Instinct never goes wrong.

> And Reason raise o'er Instinct as you can,
> In this 'tis God directs, in that 'tis Man.
> (97-8)

Instinct, he declares, is what causes each creature to find a mate, then tend to their young, so that self-love extends wider and wider to take in more and more of society.

In defending the claims of Instinct, Pope describes how life was lived in earliest times – in a "state of nature". Man, it seems, was a vegetarian then. He didn't kill his fellow animals and he certainly didn't sacrifice them in religious rituals. "Ah! how unlike the man of times to come!" (161)

But a serious problem creeps in almost unnoticed here. If "Whatever IS, is RIGHT", then it must *always* have been right, but that cannot be if things were once better, and if they were better once, then they cannot be perfect now. Pope's whole system looks to be in danger of falling apart, but the liveliness of the verse and the fascination of the detail blinds us to the fallacies. Reason, we now learn, was taught by Instinct; it was how man learned the arts he now practises. From the birds and beasts we learned what was safe to eat. From the bees we learned how to build; from the moles to plough, and from the silkworm to weave. We even learned politics: "The ant's republic and the realm of bees". It is all so delightful that for a moment we might fail to see how silly it is!

Veneration of the head of the family in those far-off times led to the belief in "One great first Father". But again we find that things went badly wrong. Leaders became tyrants; gods and fiends were propitiated on marble altars reeking with gore. Where could we look for salvation from such a state of affairs? Self-love is the answer. Universal self-love is what causes the majority to bind together to restrain the tyrant:

> All join to guard what each desires to gain,
> Forc'd into virtue thus by Self-defence,
> Ev'n Kings learn'd justice and benevolence.
>
> (278-80)

Concordia discors, which we met earlier, seems also to be at the root of it:

> Till jarring int'rests of themselves create
> Th'according music of a well-mix'd State.
>
> (293-4)

The overall optimism is so starry-eyed, we are told that:

> For forms of Government let fools contest;
> Whate'er is best administer'd is best
>
> (303-4)

Now admittedly Pope did not have before him the examples of what Stalin's administration achieved, nor the atrocities committed by the meticulous administrative machinery of Nazi Germany, but it is still hard to believe that some moment's historical reflection (Rome?) would not have dented such a theory, or that "All Mankind's concern is Charity". (308)

This Epistle ends on the kind of Tremendous Chord which Handel favoured:

> Thus God and Nature link'd the gen'ral frame,
> And bade Self-love and Social be the same.
>
> (317-8)

That little word *Thus* may be trying to persuade us that we have reached this conclusion through a process of logic, but some of the steps have taken us along some rather uncertain and circuitous routes.

In a poem which is so against-all-the-odds optimistic, it is only to be expected that the final Epistle should be about *Happiness*. It is, says Pope, "our being's end and aim!" (1) But once again he reminds us that "the Universal Cause/Acts not by partial, but by gen'ral laws" (35-6), adding that it

> ... makes what Happiness we justly call
> Subsist not in the good of one, but all.
>
> (37-8)

Following this line of thought, we are obliged to accept that there must be inequalities; some will be richer than others, and so true happiness cannot lie in external and material things. "Bliss is the same in subject or in King" (58), we are told and that the balance is achieved by *hope* and *fear*. Those who have nothing live in hope, while those who have an abundance live in fear that they may lose it. If this *balance* seems hard to credit, there are even odder arguments to follow.

Happiness, he goes on to state, lies in three words: Health, Peace and Competence (80) – the last meaning enough to live on. "Health consists with Temperance alone" (81) he states bluntly and then goes on to consider peace. Can he, a migraine sufferer with his growth stunted and his spine curved by Pott's disease, *really* have believed this?

Peace comes from *Virtue*, and while bad people might seem to prosper, they will never have what they want, which is "to pass for good". (92) Again the emptiness of the thinking is itself shocking. Consider Hitler again. To his dying day, he believed his people adored him as their saviour, and plenty did.

And what of the good people – and Pope cites some examples – who seem to gain no reward for their goodness and indeed sometimes suffer disaster? The answer is that it is folly to expect God to alter His general laws in favour of particulars.

And what kind of reward would Virtue expect? Were it to be something material, then what would seem enough? No, "The soul's calm sunshine; and the heart-felt joy" (168) is Virtue's prize. So all this reasoning seems to have led us to the cliché that virtue is its own reward.

It then takes Pope eighty lines and more to dismiss *honour, titles, greatness, fame* and *wisdom* as all being of no true worth and ending with a brief list of those who have achieved such things but have scarcely benefited – Cromwell for example "damn'd to everlasting fame." (284)

Recalling what he had said in Epistle III of the ability of self-love to expand to include others, Pope again uses the image of widening ripples when a pebble is thrown into a lake, until it takes "ev'ry creature in, of ev'ry kind" (370).

The poem had begun with an invocation to St. John Bolingbroke and ends appropriately with an encomium in which Pope calls him his guide, philosopher and friend. It used to be said that he had provided Pope with many of his ideas but this is now thought to be unlikely.

The closing lines are a remarkably compact summary of the ideas which the poem has covered. It has

> Shew'd erring Pride, WHATEVER IS, IS RIGHT;
> That REASON, PASSION, answer one great aim;
> That true SELF-LOVE and SOCIAL are the same;
> That VIRTUE only makes our Bliss below;
> And all our knowledge is, OURSELVES TO KNOW.

But what are we to make of it all? Thomas de Quincey seems to encapsulate the problem: "If the question were asked, 'What ought to have been the best of Pope's poems?', most people would answer the *Essay on Man*. If the question were asked, 'What is the worst?' all people would say the *Essay on Man*."

It is certainly true that the *Essay* had the potential to be a great poem. The themes are those which have always concerned us: Why did God create the universe? Why is there evil in the world? Why does God allow natural disasters to overwhelm us? Why do the evil prosper and the good so often seem to fail? Is there an afterlife and what will it be like? There are also some passages of great poetry, but it has to be said, not enough of them.

Johnson was ambivalent about it. He could appreciate the poetic skill, but when it came to the ideas his criticism cracked like a whip. "Never were penury of knowledge and vulgarity of sentiment so happily disguised." But against this we have the voice of Voltaire insisting that it was "le premier des poèmes didactiques" and if proof were needed of how powerfully it spoke to the people of the 18th century we have only to consider the number of times it was translated in the century following its publication: German 24 times, French 16, Italian 18, Polish five, Swedish four, Latin five, Dutch six. And there were also versions in Czech, Danish, Hungarian, Icelandic, Portuguese, Romanian, Russian, Spanish, Turkish and Welsh. It is difficult to argue against that.

7

Moral Essays

Although the four poems to be considered in this chapter are known collectively as the *Moral Essays*, this was not the title Pope gave them, nor was it one which was used in his own lifetime. To him, they were always *Epistles to Several Persons*. It was William Warburton who first made the change in his nine-volume edition of Pope's *Collected Works* in 1751, and for some reason it is a title which has stuck.

Moral Essays was always a misnomer and shows a fundamental failure to understand what the poems are. They are not didactic essays in the way of the *Essay on Man*; their tone is far more relaxed, as indeed a letter should be. The epistle was an accepted and totally different literary form – stemming largely from Horace – an easy-going exchange of views, sometimes of gossip, between friends, and so, of course, each of these poems is shaped both in style and content to suit the person to whom it is addressed.

The first is to Lord Cobham. Cobham had had a distinguished military career, rising to the rank of lieutenant general under Marlborough. He then became a prominent member of the Whig government for many years, but resigned and formed an opposition party when Walpole refused to allow an enquiry into the scandal of the South Sea Company. After that, landscape gardening became one of his passions and he created the magnificent garden at Stowe where Pope was a frequent summer visitor.

The sub-title of this first Epistle is 'Of the Knowledge and Characters of Men' and while the majority of the examples and references are to males, women do make an appearance, so 'Men', in this instance, must again be regarded as a generic term.

Much of the thinking in the poem seems to stem from Pope's reading of Montaigne's *Essays*, and especially 'Of the Inconstancy of Our Actions' which stresses the difficulty of even trying to understand human nature. Appropriately, therefore, it begins with a contradiction. Cobham, having been a soldier, politician and man of the world, would, Pope suggests, have little time for the *bookish* approach someone like himself might be suspected of taking. Cobham's attitude would probably be far more practical: *judge a fellow by his actions*. But neither way – neither empirical nor rational – Pope argues, would get to the core of the problem. Our own prejudices will often colour our judgements and, besides, people are changing all the time you are trying to study them:

> Our depths who fathoms, or our shallows finds,
> Quick whirls, and shifting eddies, of our minds?
>
> (29-30)

> Like following life thro' creatures you dissect,
> You lose it in the moment you detect.
>
> (39-40)

And how can we hope to understand other people's minds when we cannot understand our own, he asks, when our apparent motives may be dictated by our subconscious? *Subconscious*, of course, was not a term which existed in Pope's day, but it does seem to be what he is suggesting when he says:

> When Sense subsides, and Fancy sports in sleep,
> (Tho' past the recollection of the thought)
> Becomes the stuff of which our dream is wrought:
> Something as dim to our internal view,
> Is thus, perhaps, the cause of most we do.
>
> (46-50)

Most people will tend, like Cobham, to judge from appearances – "Infer the Motive from the Deed" (53) but again there might be many causes which are far from apparent. A man might "be sick, in love, or had not din'd" (80). We also make the mistake of assessing people by their social standing or their profession, whereas this is clearly no safe guide. People are a mass of contradictions and the only thing which is unchanging, he concludes, is our *Ruling Passion* (174) a theory which he had developed in detail in Epistle II of an *Essay on Man*. Johnson was later to dismiss it out of hand. "The doctrine is in itself pernicious as well as false: its tendency is to produce the belief of a kind of moral predestination, or overriding principle which cannot be resisted." And while Pope added the proviso that such a Passion always needed to be guided by our Reason, that still does not seem to detract from what Johnson says.

Up to this point the tone of the Epistle has been somewhat reminiscent of the *Essay on Man*. The mists of abstraction which had sometimes tended to obscure the thinking there had not totally blown away, but there is a marked change when Pope begins to introduce us to real people, the first being Philip, Duke of Wharton, who certainly was the embodiment of contradictions and wasted opportunities. His grandfather had fought on the side of Parliament at the Battle of Edge Hill. His father had been influential in the Revolution of 1688 and Philip himself had displayed such early brilliance in the Whig government that George I had created a dukedom for him when he was only 19. Yet within a few years he had become a Roman Catholic, a fanatical Jacobite and had joined the Pretender in France. That did not last and he seems then to have wandered the Continent, squandering a fortune and getting drunk, eventually dying in a monastery in Catalonia while still only in his early thirties. Contradictions enough, which Pope, unconvincingly, to my mind, puts down to his *Lust for Praise*.

The *Ruling Passion*, he goes on to say, is our one constant factor and remains with us until the moment of our death and to prove this he ends the Epistle with a series of brilliant vignettes. Among them we have an old lecher who "crawls on knocking knees" to his mistress; an actress with a horror of being buried in a woollen shroud, and insisting on chintz, and Brussels lace. "One would not, sure, be frightful when one's dead." And my own favourite:

> The Courtier smooth, who forty years had shin'd
> An humble servant to all human kind,
> Just brought out this, when scarce his tongue could stir,
> 'If – where I'm going – I could serve you, Sir?'
> (252-5)

The closing four lines are a tribute to Cobham, who had been prepared to sacrifice his military position and his place in the government for his principles. His patriotism being his Ruling Passion, Pope speculates that his dying words would be "Oh, save my country, Heav'n". And these lines are still to be seen at Stowe, engraved on the pillar his widow had engraved in his memory.

Epistle II is entitled 'To a Lady', and sub-titled 'Of the Characters of Women'. Although it does not say so, Pope acknowledged that the lady in question was Martha Blount. Martha and her sister Teresa came from a long-established family of Roman Catholic gentry and had first met Pope at Binfield when all three were still in their teens. Pope wrote several mildly flirtatious letters to them and later there were rumours that Martha was his mistress. Some even claimed she was his wife, but there is no evidence to support either suggestion. What is certain is that his friendship with Martha was the strongest and most lasting of his whole life and when he died he left her £1,000, all his "goods and chattels" and a lifelong interest in the rest of his estate.

The closeness of their relationship can be felt in the poem itself. Its opening lines suggest that we are overhearing them in the middle of a conversation, a conversation which seems to be taking place in an imaginary art gallery and Pope is remarking on the various portraits of women which hang there. The overall theme of this Epistle is inconstancy and as he points out there is not simply one portrait of each woman, but, as was fashionable at the time, several and in several different guises:

> How many Pictures of one Nymph we view,
> All how unlike each other, all how true!
>
> (5-6)

There is a portrait of a countess resplendent in her ermine robes and alongside it another of the same lady dressed as a simple shepherdess. Another is shown first with her husband and then, naked, as Leda being raped by Zeus in the guise of a swan. A third is represented, sweetly, as St Cecelia and then, seductively, as Mary Magdalene. Which of these portraits could be said to be the real woman? Perhaps none. Perhaps all are equally deceptive, affected and hypocritical.

Pope, we remind ourselves, studied painting under his friend Charles Jervas and in this gallery he is not only a guide but a painter too and one who knows exactly how these likenesses should be caught:

> Pictures like these, dear Madam, to design,
> Asks no firm hand, and no unerring line;
> Some wandering touch, or some reflected light,
> Some flying stroke alone can hit 'em right.
>
> (151-4)

And in some flying strokes there follow a few brief portraits which do exactly that. We have the slovenly *Sappho* (probably intended to be Lady Mary Wortley Montagu) putting on her make-up – "her toilet's greasy task". And fickle *Papillia* (Latin for a butterfly)

> wedded to her doating spark,
> Sighs for the shades – 'How charming is a Park!'
> A Park is purchas'd, but the Fair he sees
> All bath'd in tears – 'Oh, odious, odious Trees!'
>
> (37-40)

Pope's mastery of the couplet is now such that he can manage the distinctive sound of a speaking voice within the relaxed and colloquial tone of the personal epistle.

We may laugh at the foibles of the Papillias of this world, but the portraits which follow grow increasingly dark:

> Narcissa's nature, tolerably mild,
> To make a wash, would hardly stew a child.
>
> (52-3)

Her nature is in fact an ugly mixture of seeming benevolence and blatant vice – one moment reading books of divinity and the next getting drunk with the likes of Francis Chartres, a man notorious for all kinds of villainy from cheating at cards to rape. She is followed by Philomedé who publicly preaches *Delicacy* and *Taste*, but in private will bed anyone, including her footmen.

Then we come to the notorious portrait of Atossa. The actual name is that of the wife and sister of a mad and drunken king of Persia – facts which ought to warn us of what is to come. It is an alarming picture of a sixty-year-old woman given to terrible paroxysms of rage; a megalomaniac bordering on insanity; hating almost everyone around her and roundly hated by them in return.

> From loveless youth to unrespected age,
> No Passion gratify'd except her Rage.
>
>   *   *   *
>
> Offend her, and she knows not to forgive;
> Oblige her, and she'll hate you while you live.
>
> (125-6 & 137-8)

These portraits have, not surprisingly, upset a number of feminist critics, but perhaps they are a little mistaken in their reaction. Pope was no woman hater. Women fascinated him, as we can see from *The*

Rape of the Lock. It is not women in general he is portraying here; these are portraits of a particular type – wealthy, aristocratic women who wielded a good deal of social power. They are the type of woman one meets in some of the novels of Henry James or the plays of Oscar Wilde. No one could surely consider Lady Bracknell to be representative of women in *general*. The social scene has changed greatly in the 21st century. Wealthy, aristocratic women still exist, but they no longer have the social dominance they once had. Instead we now have *Celebrities*: glamorous young women who seem to be famous simply for being famous – having been seen on television – but with no obvious talent for anything. Their lifestyle invites ridicule, but such ridicule has no bearing on the vast majority of women and this is surely true of Pope's day too. It is significant, I think, that he did not give these women real names. What would be the point? The individuals come and go, but the type remains and in some instances is still recognisable today. I could suggest contemporary names to fit them, but they would in all likelihood have become forgotten before I had finished writing the next chapter. As Pope put it, "Alive ridiculous, and dead, forgot!" (248)

In the footnotes to the critical editions of Pope's *Satires* we find literary scholars suggesting who the actual people were whom Pope had in mind. It is probably an interesting guessing game to play, but means nothing to us unless we have an extensive knowledge of 18th-century social history. For example, was Atossa the Duchess of Marlborough or the Duchess of Buckinghamshire? Expert opinions differ. But if it could be proven, one way or the other, what difference would it make to our reading of the poem? It might be wiser, I suggest, to accept that Atossa was an horrendously alarming woman with a blazing temper. She existed once and probably still exists somewhere, though if we are lucky we will not meet her.

It would be foolish to pretend that Pope's attitude to women is totally defensible. It is not, and certainly not when it comes to his view of their *Ruling Passions*:

> In Men, we various Ruling Passions find,
> In Women, two almost divide the kind;
> Those, only fix'd, they first or last obey,
> The Love of Pleasure, and the Love of Sway.
>
> (207-10)

– later asserting that "ev'ry Woman is at heart a Rake" and that "ev'ry Lady would be Queen for Life". But he does at least acknowledge the part that "Man's oppression" plays in this, and one can detect some feeling of compassion for the Belindas caught up in the marriage market, and for what they may become in superannuated old age:

> See how the World its Veterans rewards!
> A Youth of frolicks, an old Age of Cards,
> Fair to no purpose, artful to no end,
> Young without Lovers, old without a Friend,
> A Fop their Passion, but their Prize a Sot,
> Alive, ridiculous, and dead, forgot!
>
> (243-8)

At last he turns again to Martha Blount, who in contrast to all that has gone before, embodies his ideal. He compares her with the serenity of the moon rather than the glare and dazzle of the sun. It is her inner qualities he singles out for praise – her ability "To raise the thought and touch the heart" (250). She too of course has her inconsistencies, but they are perhaps more what Shakespeare meant by "infinite variety". She combines the best qualities to be found in men and women. Heaven, he says, "Shakes all together and produces – You." The qualities he admires and values in Martha are those which Clarissa had argued for at the close of *The Rape of the Lock* and the Epistle concludes:

> the world shall know it,
> To you gave Sense, Good-humour and a Poet.
>
> (291-2)

Pope made many enemies in his life and would attack them ferociously, but his capacity for true and lasting friendship should not be forgotten. One of his close friends was Allen, Lord Bathurst, a loud, rumbustious man with appetites as large as himself. He was the father of 17 legitimate children – all by the same wife – yet is also said to have been an incorrigible womaniser, and though he also ate and drank to excess, he lived to be 91. Again landscape gardening was the passion he and Pope shared and it was Bathurst who once threatened to send a cart to scoop up Pope's whole house and garden and carry it off to Cirencester if he didn't come and visit him.

The sub-title of the 'Epistle to Bathurst' is 'Of the Use of Riches' but it might as well have been the *Mis-use* of Riches, as Pope's attack is aimed at the rise of capitalism and the new money-men in the City of London, the merchants, investors and stock-jobbers who were wresting power from the traditional landed gentry, and whose mis-use of the money-market had led to scandals such as the South Sea Bubble.

At the outset, Bathurst is given the role of a cynic and made to argue that the gods gave gold to man as some kind of cosmic joke "to keep the fools in play" (5) whereas Pope claims that Heaven has arranged that there are two kinds of men, "To squander these, and those to hide again" and that these two extremes will balance each other out.

We see very early in the poem that there will be a strong religious and political element in it when he states that wealth has been awarded indiscriminately and is "No grace of Heav'n or token of th'Elect". The Elect were the Puritans who, following Calvin, believed that material success in life was a mark of virtue and that poverty was inflicted as a punishment for sin. Pope counters this with the obvious fact that wealth is acquired both by the good and the evil. He grants that gold allows us to buy "the Needs of life" (27) but it can also be used to hire a killer, and while it facilitates trade, it also "lures the Pyrate". (32)

In a whimsical passage he speculates on how difficult corruption would be if, instead of money, we still relied on barter. It would be all too obvious if the politician's bribe arrived as a "thousand jars of oil" or "a hundred oxen". And what would become of gambling if a Lord turned up at his Club leading a prize bull and went home with "six whores"?

In contrast there was now the new paper-credit, the Bank of England having introduced bank notes in 1693 and so lent "Corruption lighter wings to fly" (70). Money brings access to the necessities of life, but great wealth does not, as Pope's examples show, bring happiness. Indeed it can lead to a total lack of Christian charity:

> Perhaps you think the Poor might have their part?
> Bond damns the Poor and hates them from his heart;
> The grave Sir Gilbert holds it for a rule,
> That every man in want is knave or fool;
>
> (100-4)

The Ruling Passion now puts in another of its varied appearances, this time in the form of a duality in which miserliness is followed by extravagance, and it is this, Pope believes, which keeps money in circulation. An odd belief, but one he supports by the story of Old Cotta and his profligate son who squanders every penny his father had hoarded and ends up bankrupt. It is an obvious enough antithesis, but in the description of Old Cotta's house, silent and overgrown with weeds, we recognise the opposite of the tradition of the Country House poem, a tradition exemplified by Ben Jonson's *To Penshurst*, which celebrated not only the grandeur and beauty of the house and its gardens but extolled its owner's generosity in entertaining guests, offering patronage to artists and giving freely to the local poor. Here were aristocrats with a social awareness. In Old Cotta's house there is

> Silence without, and Fasts within the wall,
> No rafter'd roofs with dance and tabor sound,
> No noon-tide bell invites the country round.
>
> (190-2)

The rich, Pope is saying, have a responsibility to use their wealth for the general well-being and not just to satisfy their own selfishness. Bathurst "unspoil'd by wealth", is praised for his generosity, but there are others with far less means who also set an example, and Pope cites the man of Ross, John Kyrle, to give him his real name, who managed, with an income of only £500 a year, to bring running water down into the town of Ross in Herefordshire, build almshouses and a shady public walk on a hill overlooking the River Wye. As Pope presents him to us, settling disputes, healing the sick, and feeding the poor, he is clearly meant to exemplify the Christian duties which are incumbent on all believers, rich or poor, but wisely he does not overemphasise the point.

In contrast Pope then gives us a picture of the gross abuse of money: the thousands of pounds lavished on the funeral of a miser. And in added contrast to that he paints the grisly death scene of George Villiers, the second Duke of Buckingham, who had once had an income of £50,000 a year, had been a favourite of Charles II, yet died in squalor in Yorkshire:

> In the worst inn's worst room, with mat half-hung,
> The floors of plaister, and the walls of dung

On once a flock-bed, but repair'd with straw,
With tape-ty'd curtains, never meant to draw,
Great Villiers lies

(299-305)

The detail here is so exact, so precise and yet so economically presented.

Pope briefly wonders what will happen to such people when they die, but avoids the issue by suggesting that Bathurst must be tired by now and so offers to tell him a story. The story is that of Sir Balaam – the name is that of an Old Testament figure who "loved the ways of unrighteousness". At the outset Sir Balaam is a "plain good man" whom the Devil decides to have for his own. Having failed to win Job from God with suffering and hardship, Satan, "wiser than of yore", makes him rich instead. A few fortunate 'wrecks' off the Cornish coast, some shady dealings over a stolen diamond, and Sir Balaam is on the way up. He is too busy now to go to church at all, but his wife does; catches a cold there and dies. A new wife "of quality" appears and before long he has left the City and is at Court, and then in parliament. But his wife runs up such debts that he takes a bribe, is found out, impeached and hanged:

The Devil and the King divide the prize,
And sad Sir Balaam curses God and dies.

(401-2)

The story is told with such verve it is almost Chaucerian, but with more than a touch of Hogarth to it. Whereas the satirical portraits in the 'Epistle to a Lady', vivid though they were, tended to be static, there is now narrative and pace.

The Fourth Epistle, also entitled 'Of the use of Riches', is addressed to Richard Boyle, Earl of Burlington, a truly remarkable man. Seven years younger than Pope, he had spent much of his youth in Italy where he had developed a lifelong passion for the work of the Venetian architect Andrea Palladio. Such was his influence when he returned to this country and published a book of the Italian's designs that it is Burlington who is credited with having established that Palladian symmetry and simplicity which is the mark of the finest Georgian architecture.

When a second edition of this Epistle was published Pope added a half-title 'Of False Taste' and it cannot have been accidental that twice in the first 16 lines he rhymes *taste* with *waste*, as he describes for us the gaudy extravagancies that the nouveaux riches of his day (and we might pause here to think of our own stars and celebrities) were having built; in some cases lavishing money on projects simply to show how rich they were. Conspicuous consumption is clearly nothing new, but as he points out:

> Something there is more needful than Expense,
> And something previous e'en to Taste – 'tis Sense.
>
> (41-2)

Following on from this we have three paragraphs in which Pope sets out in brief his own ideas on landscape gardening. His guiding principle was always "Consult the Genius of the Place" (57) by which he meant that a garden should never be forced onto a landscape; rather it should be adapted to fit in with the countryside around it. And when he says, "In all, let Nature never be forgot" we are reminded of a similar assertion in the *Essay on Criticism* "First follow NATURE and your Judgement frame by her just Standard which is still the same". And we realise that his views on gardening and poetry are all of a piece. When he uses the word Nature, he has in mind those qualities which Newton had revealed in the natural world – the universal principles of order and harmony. What Pope is advocating in a garden is the same blend of grandeur and simplicity which we hear in the heroic couplet and which in its turn the inherent balance of the couplet is best able to demonstrate.

When these principles are followed, Pope says, you may end up with "A Work to wonder at", adding, with a compliment to his friend, Lord Cobham, "perhaps a Stowe".

To demonstrate the total opposite of Stowe, Pope takes his readers on a tour of *Timon's Villa*. This was once taken to be meant for his friend the Duke of Chando's estate at Cannons, a suggestion which upset them both.

Pope insisted that it was not and recent scholarship has shown that it could not have been.

Timon has done everything on the grandest possible scale and the result is ostentatious vulgarity: "His pond an ocean, his parterre a Down" (106). It is so vast that he himself is dwarfed by the enormousness of it all. A north wind comes howling through it so that

> Who but must laugh, the Master when he sees,
> A puny insect, shiv'ring at a breeze!
>
> (107-8)

Pope had once put it to Spence that, "All the rules of gardening are reducible to three heads: the contrasts, the management of surprises, and the concealment of the bounds." Timon's garden fails on all three counts, and what is worse it sports something Pope could not abide – topiary, "Trees cut to Statues", and "Statues thick as Trees".

Indoors is as bad. Everything is for show. In the library it is the binding of the books his lordship boasts of. He doesn't open them. In fact the top shelves are of wood, painted to *look* like books. His Chapel is luxurious – inappropriately so. The ceiling is painted with a "sprawl" of saints. The music is more of a jig and after all the *Pride of Pray'r* the sermon is preached by a *soft Dean* who is far too polite ever to mention Hell. The dining room is equally vast and uninviting and Pope concludes:

> I curse such lavish cost, and little skill,
> And swear no Day was ever pass'd so ill.
>
> (167-8)

Looking on the bright side, and true to his belief that evil can often lead to good, Pope admits that it at least keeps a lot of people in employment, and looks forward to a time in the future when it will all have disappeared, as indeed it has.

As the poem draws to a close, Pope asks and then answers a question:

> Who then shall grace, or who improve the Soil?
> Who plants like BATHURST, or who builds like BOYLE.
>
> (177-8)

Joining the names of his two friends, he says that men like these look after their tenants, and their estates are not just for selfish grandeur and show. Even their trees provide timber for future navies. And in lines which recall the optimism of *Windsor-Forest* he sees Burlington inspiring a whole host of much-needed public works – harbours, roads, bridges. The very last line "These are Imperial Works, and worthy Kings" may be a silent tribute to Burlington as it recalls a line in Dryden's *Aeneid*, "These are imperial arts, and worthy thee".

When we look back over these four Epistles, a clear line of development can be seen. The first, 'To Cobham', still shows a keen interest in those philosophical speculations which occupied Pope in the *Essay on Man*, but abstraction then gives way to a consideration of actualities. Not at first actual people, however, but composite, generalised portraits of certain clearly recognised types. Then, as his vision narrows and concentrates, so real names do appear: Lord Wharton, the forger John Ward, and Chartres the swindler. And while the 'Epistle to Burlington' relies on classical tags and labels, its central topic is one which is urgent and practical and of the greatest personal concern to Pope. It is also the most Horatian in tone and so looks forward to the *Satires* which are soon to follow.

It is all so tidy, it is a pity it isn't true. The fact is that the 'Epistle to Burlington' was written first, as early as 1731 – even before an *Essay on Man*. 'To Bathurst' appeared in 1733, 'To Cobham' in 1734 and the last to be written was 'To a Lady' in 1735. Literature itself, sadly, is not as tidy as literary criticism would have it – and yet … The order in which Pope chose to publish them as a sequence could suggest that this may be the direction he wanted his work to be seen as taking. Perhaps we can have it both ways.

8
Imitations of Horace

Although the addressees of the *Moral Essays* were all friends of Pope, they were not his closest friends. These were Jonathan Swift, John Gay of *The Beggar's Opera* fame, the poet and scholar Thomas Parnell, who had assisted him with his translation of Homer, and Dr John Arbuthnot. Together they made up the *Scriblerus Club*, which mocked and satirised the second-rate writers they regarded as cluttering up the literary scene.

Arbuthnot, a "tall, slouching Scot, fond of literature and practical jokes", was personal physician to Queen Anne, and the least literary of the group, but there was no one whose friendship Pope more valued and he was clearly moved when Arbuthnot, nearing death and only too aware of it, wrote to him in July 1734, urging him as a "Last Request" to "continue that noble Disdain and Abhorrence of Vice, which you seem naturally endu'd with." Pope's immediate response was the poem which Warburton called *The Prologue to the Satires*, but which we know as the *Epistle to Dr Arbuthnot*. It was published in January 1735, the month before Arbuthnot died.

It is easy to see why Warburton gave it the title he did. Following in the tradition of Horace and Juvenal, Pope can be seen as constructing his own 'Defence of Satire', and although he calls it an *Epistle*, it is in some ways more in the tradition of Horace's *Satires*; the most obvious connection being that Arbuthnot himself speaks in what is ostensibly a letter *to* him. Likewise the opening is more dramatic than epistolary:

> Shut, shut the door, good *John*! fatigu'd I said,
> Tye up the knocker, say I'm sick, I'm dead,
> The Dog-star rages! nay 'tis past a doubt,
> All *Bedlam*, or *Parnassus*, is let out.
>
> (1-4)

The *John* in this instance is his servant John Serle; he would never have addressed Arbuthnot so.

He is besieged by a plague of poetasters. They follow him to Twickenham, forcing their way into his garden, seeking him out even

74

in his grotto. Nowhere is he safe from them, neither on the river nor in his carriage. They even pester him in church. This of course only serves to confirm his fame, his celebrity status and this is part of the purpose of the poem. As a satirist he needs to create a persona for himself – someone his readers will sympathise with, whom they will like and so believe. As he explains in the preliminary Advertisement, he did not want to go into print on this matter at all, but was prompted to not only by the attacks on his work (that he could accept) but attacks on his 'Person, Morals and Family'. He is not the aggressor, he is saying, he is the victim.

And those people who profess their admiration and their friendship for him do not mean it. They all want him to *do* something for them to advance themselves. He cannot keep silent about this state of affairs; he must speak out against them, he says, and he shows his contempt in a brilliant metaphor which again takes up the insect image:

> Who shames a Scribler? break one cobweb thro',
> He spins the slight, self-pleasing thread anew;
> Destroy his Fib, or Sophistry; in vain,
> The Creature's at his dirty work again;
>
> (89-92)

But when he begins to name names, Arbuthnot moves in and advises caution, "… learn prudence of a friend. I too could write and I am twice as tall." (102-3) Pope allows himself to be calmed down and at line 25 the poem changes direction. As he has just told us that he has been driven to speak out, so he now justifies his position by explaining that it seems to have been what he was born to do. In the account of his life which follows, there is a good deal of self-aggrandisement. His initial image, that he was "Dipt … in ink" (125-6) reminds us of Achilles, the hero, being dipped into the River Styx by Thetis, his mother, to make him invulnerable. And there is a blatant appeal to our sympathy when he says his writing has helped him to get through "this long disease, my life". (132)

Countering the charge that he might have been born to write, but didn't have to publish, he lists the names of all those who encouraged him, and it is a long and eminent list. Some of the early names – Granville, Garth and Walsh – may mean little to us today, but it goes on to include Congreve and Swift and even manages to bring in Dryden:

Happy my Studies, when by these approv'd!
Happier their Author, when by these belov'd!
                                                    (143-4)

Modesty was never one of his failings.

His writing career began, he explains, with pastorals, at which no one could "take offence". Dennis did of course, but Pope ignored him, or so he says, which is not strictly true. One can sense his blood pressure rise however when he remembers the attacks made by Bentley and Theobald on his Homer and his edition of Shakespeare:

Yet ne'er one sprig of Laurel grac'd these ribalds,
From slashing *Bentley* down to pidling *Tibalds*.
                                                    (163-4)

These are little men. They are not creative minds and he is able to dismiss them with one of the most memorable of his insect metaphors:

Ev'n such small Critics some regard may claim,
Preserv'd in *Milton's* or in *Shakespeare's* name.
Pretty! in Amber to observe the forms
Of hairs, or straws, or dirt, or grubs, or worms;
The things, we know, are neither rich nor rare,
But wonder how the Devil they got there?
                                                    (167-72)

He then admits to having written a little "modest satire" which some took such exception to that it was beginning to be said, "not ADDISON himself was safe". A sly way of ensuring that the lines about *Atticus* which followed could not fail to be seen as referring directly to Addison. Strangely, the portrait which Pope gives us is both a warm tribute and at the same time a scathing denunciation – the man is:

Blest with each Talent and each Art to please,
And born to write, converse, and live with ease.
                                                    (195-6)

But he is also so self-centred he cannot tolerate or acknowledge ability or achievement in anybody else. Such is his devious nature, however, he would never openly voice his feelings and so make enemies. Instead he denigrates and destroys reputations by insinuation. Here, once again, we see how the nature of the couplet contributes to the effect and to the meaning. The antithesis and the balance of eight words tell us what might take a novelist whole paragraphs. Atticus will, "Damn with faint praise, assent with civil leer". And what eight words they are! The sound of the long vowel in *leer* is itself so very expressive, but there is also the hiss which precedes it – *civil leer*. And in the next line he rhymes it with *sneer*, a word which automatically curls the lip. And when we are told that he will "Just hint a fault, and hesitate dislike" those aspirates are heard enacting for us that damning hesitation.

But Pope is still willing to conclude with the lines:

> Who but must laugh, if such a man there be?
> Who would not weep if *Atticus* were he!
>
> (213-4)

acknowledging, it would seem, the tragedy of such wasted ability.

The money Pope had made from his edition of Homer meant that he was financially independent – probably the first full-time writer ever to be so. He needed no patron, and certainly not of the type he gives us in his portrait of *Bufo*. Latin for a *toad*, Bufo, puffed up by his own vanity, gladly accepts the fulsome dedications and grovelling flattery, but gives little or nothing in return.

Pope rejoices in his independence. He is free "to see what friends, and read what books I please" (264). And by this time a reader might have noticed how many times the words *friend* and *friendship* are used in this poem: ten times in the first 266 lines. Friendship is indeed one of the chief underlying themes of the poem. "Friend to my life!" was how Pope addressed Arbuthnot at the outset.

When Pope uses the word *friendship* there is an element of moral idealism in it. It is indicative of a range of positive social values such as honesty and sincerity. Ethically it is the capacity to rate virtue higher than material success. The abuse of friendship therefore is an evil, an evil which he equates with the self-interest and political corruption of the time.

Atticus is clearly incapable of true friendship. Bufo is a worse case. He is contemptuous of those around him, and their professed friendship is only feigned.

But it is in the third portrait, that of *Sporus*, that we see the full possibility of this evil. Sporus, as contemporary readers instantly guessed, was the Whig MP, Lord Hervey. A close friend of Queen Caroline and Walpole's most trusted agent in the palace, he was their go-between and as such involved in most of the intrigues and corruption in both court and parliament. He was a close friend also of Lady Mary Wortley Montagu and when she fell out with Pope he helped her write a series of scurrilous verses, cursing him and mocking his deformity:

> But as thou hatest, be thou hated by Mankind,
> And with the Emblem of thy crooked Mind,
> Mark'd on thy Back, like *Cain* by God's own Hand,
> Wander like him, accursed through the Land.

Arbuthnot steps in to insist that Sporus is not worth bothering about. "Who breaks a Butterfly upon a Wheel?" he asks. But this sets off in Pope's mind another of those insect images. Sporus is not a butterfly, he is a bug. But this isn't enough. Within the space of two dozen lines, Pope goes from butterfly to bug, to dog, to toad, to snake.

The real life Sporus was one of Nero's favourite eunuchs; in fact he married him. The name therefore neatly combines Hervey's insidious position at court with his notorious bi-sexuality. He was in some respects a glamorous figure, but Pope will not even allow him that:

> Yet let me flap this Bug with gilded Wings,
> This painted Child of Dirt that stinks and stings.
>
> (309-10)

He is gilded and painted; it is only superficial, underneath is the dirt. He may be Walpole's puppet, but his influence at court is evil and the image changes to that of Satan whispering into the ear of Eve. There is nothing whatsoever trustworthy about the "Amphibious Thing" (326), and this is especially so of his sexuality:

> His Wit all see-saw between *that* and *this*,
> Now high, now low, now Master up, now Miss,
> And he himself one vile Antithesis.
> Amphibious Thing! that acting either Part,
> The trifling Head, or the corrupted Heart!
> Fop at the Toilet, Flatt'rer at the Board,
> Now trips a Lady, and now struts a Lord.
>
> (324-9)

Antithesis and alliteration combine in an unforgettable picture which constitutes one of the most devastating personal attacks in all literature.

Reverting now to his own life story Pope tells us, not surprisingly, that if his work has pleased it has done so by "manly ways". He has never, he says, been driven by ambition, written for money (again not strictly true) or followed fashion, and seeming to refer to the changes which took place in his writing between *The Rape of the Lock* and the *Satires*, he says:

> That not in Fancy's Maze he wander'd long,
> But stooped to Truth, and moraliz'd his song.
>
> (340-1)

And despite the criticism and abuse he has had to put up with, he remains on the side of 'fair virtue' and will expose Vice wherever he finds it without fear or favour.

This poem, which began in a tone of exasperation and which has had its fortissimo moments, quietens to a calm in which he holds up for us the picture of his father, a man who combined honour with humility, a man of temperance and innate wisdom. These, in contrast to so much that has gone before, are the ideals Pope is advocating. "O, Friend!" he addresses Arbuthnot in the final paragraph, and we see that these are the qualities and virtues he heralds under that word. In an interesting role reversal, he finally wishes he could minister to this dying physician and that in caring for his aged mother he could "rock the Cradle of reposing Age". It is a conclusion which certainly makes us feel warmly towards him, but again there is an element of special pleading here, as although Mrs Pope was alive when he wrote those words, she had been dead for 18 months when the Epistle was published.

The *Satires* and *Epistles* which follow are referred to as *Horace Imitated*. Since Wordsworth led whole generations to believe that poetry is the spontaneous overflow of powerful feelings, an *Imitation* has tended to sound like artifice, but then even *spontaneity* is itself artifice. As Yeats wisely put it:

> A line will take us hours maybe;
> Yet if it does not seem a moment's thought,
> Our stitching and unstitching has been nought.

The 17th century had been a great age of translation and much thought had been given to the practice of it. Translation as such was intended for those with little or no understanding of the original, but imitation was carried out in the belief that a reader would not only understand the original, but be so familiar with it as to recognise the variations and the play that was being made of it. To this end, Pope had the Latin text of Horace printed alongside his own. And there was also the approach adopted by Dryden when he said of Virgil that he made him "speak that kind of English, which he would have spoken had he lived in England and written to this age." The resultant interplay of similarity and disparity which *imitation* of this kind entailed had become a recognised literary genre, and one of its advantages was that Pope's criticisms and opinions looked to be backed, as it were, by the authority of Horace.

There may be fewer readers today skilled enough in Latin to read Pope in the way he would have expected his contemporaries to do, but a comparison of the opening lines of his Satire 'To Mr Fortescue' with a modern translation by Smith Palmer Bovie does at least give a flavour of what we are missing:

P.   There are, (I scarce can think it, but am told)
      There are to whom my Satire seems too bold,
      Scarce to wise *Peter* complaisant enough,
      And something said of *Chartres* much too rough.
      The lines are weak, another's pleas'd to say,
      Lord *Fanny* spins a thousand such a Day.
      Tim'rous by Nature, of the Rich in awe,
      I come to Council learned in the Law.
      You'll give me, like a Friend both sage and free,
      Advice; and (as you use) without a Fee.
F.   I'd write no more.
P.   Not write? but then I *think*,
      And for my Soul I cannot sleep a Wink.

      Horace To some, it appears, my satire is far too mean
      And strains its aesthetic bounds, whereas others find
      Whatever I write anemic, and claim that my lines
      Can be turned out a thousand a day.
      Trebatius, my friend, advise me what to do.
      Trebatius Take a rest.
      Horace And not write verses at all, you say?
      Trebatius That's what I say.
      Horace Damn it! You're probably right! But I can't get
      to sleep.

Pope's professed anxiety was caused by the furore over his 'Epistle to Burlington' when he had been accused, falsely, of insulting the Duke of Chandos. He feared a similar reaction to his 'Epistle to Bathurst' and so was getting his retaliation in first. Fortescue, like Horace's Trebatius, was a lawyer and so advises caution. Write verses in praise of the King, he suggests, that's far safer. But Pope insists that he would never attack anyone who didn't deserve it:

> Yes, while I live, no rich or noble knave
> Shall walk the World, in credit to his grave.
> TO VIRTUE ONLY and HER FRIENDS, A FRIEND.
> (119-21)

That's all very well, says the lawyer, but warns him to have a care, even so. I'm bringing "Vice to light," Pope counters, adding "Such as Sir Robert would approve – " And that makes all the difference. "The Case is alter'd – you may then proceed," is his verdict. A nice irony – the implication being that any friend of Walpole is above the law and may do as he pleases. It is, of course, only an *implication*.

For all the closeness of the imitation the tone is different from that of Horace. In his *Essay on Criticism* Pope had observed how:

> *Horace* still charms with graceful negligence
> And without Method *talks* us in to Sense,
> Will like a Friend familiarly convey
> The truest Notions in the easiest way.
> (653-6)

But there is less of that "graceful negligence" in Pope's versions. He is far more aggressive; the exception being that addressed 'To Mr Bethel' as here Pope is not so much attacking a vice as asserting particular virtues – virtues such as moderation, good sense, and a healthy lifestyle, friendship, hospitality and a care for what today we call *the wider community*. Without some such core of positive beliefs, a satire would not be a *satire*, but would degenerate into a lampoon or a libel. 'To Mr Bethel' is to be seen therefore as the touchstone against which the corruption and the depravity of society, the city the court and the government is to be measured.

The opening couplet shows what is to follow:

> What and how great, the Virtue and the Art
> To live on little with a chearful heart.

The speaker in Horace's satire is Orfellus, a yeoman farmer striving to restore his fortunes having had his lands confiscated by Octavius and given to one of his supporters, and Pope, having been forced by anti-Catholic legislation to leave his house at Binfield, must have felt some affinity with him. But it is his friend Hugh Bethel who extols the simple life. In a letter written to him in 1726 Pope had said, "I agree with you in your opinion of company and amusements, and all the silly things which mankind wou'd fain make pleasures of, when in truth they are labour and sorrow." What Bethel advocates is again the Golden Mean – that point of balance between extremes:

> Between Excess and Famine lies a mean;
> Plain, but not sordid; tho' not splendid, clean.
>
> (47-8)

It is food and the way we eat which becomes the issue on which people are judged in this poem. Some live in such deliberate miserliness that they:

> Sell their presented Partridges, and Fruits
> And humbly live on rabbits and on roots.
>
> (51-2)

And you cannot tell their wine from their vinegar. While others glut themselves to such an extent that:

> bile and wind, and phlegm, and acid jar,
> And all the Man is one intestine war.
>
> (71-2)

From individuals Pope turns to a wider social picture in which, understated but still there, is the concept of civic responsibility. Now we see the wealthy man hoarding his money, gluttonously, while the poor suffer:

> Oh Impudence of wealth! with all thy store
> How dar'st thou let one worthy man be poor?
>
> (117-8)

Having given us Bethel's views, Pope tells us that he himself tries to follow this example, even though his own *estate* is no more than five acres. He invites his friends to stay with him and share a homely meal where the food is all local produce:

To Hounslow-heath I point, and Bansted-down,
Thence comes your mutton, and these chicks my own:
(143-4)

Recalling Horace's yeoman Orfellus who had had his lands confiscated, Pope refers to the double tax he incurs as a Roman Catholic and to the property laws which had obliged his family to sell their Binfield estate:

My lands are sold, my Father's house is gone;
I'll hire another's, is not that my own?
(155-6)

But it is not something that Pope allows to bother him. What is property after all? It goes to someone else eventually:

Let Lands and Houses have what Lords they will,
Let us be fix'd, and our own Masters still.
(179-80)

As that fine 18th-century scholar Maynard Mack put it (even more succinctly than Pope), "Self-possession is the only possession that is ours to keep."

Among the main changes which were taking place in the early 18th century, the rise of the new money-men, the scriveners, lawyers and stock-jobbers clearly grated on Pope, though this did not stop him from investing in the stock-market quite assiduously himself. Nevertheless it is his hostility to all such things which gives the 'Epistle to Bolingbroke' its much sharper tone. To those earning their living in the City, Virtue was hardly a priority; indeed it was irrelevant when "A Man of wealth was dubb'd a man of Worth."

The First in Horace's First Book of Epistles was addressed to his friend and patron Maecenas and so it is only right that Pope's Imitation should be addressed to Bolingbroke – the "guide, philosopher and friend" of the *Essay on Man*. Following Horace very closely he claims he has retired from Satire. He's too old and feeble, he says, to carry on the fight:

Weak tho' I am of limb, and short of sight,
Far from a lynx, and not a Giant quite;
(49-50)

He is going to settle down and contemplate Virtue:

> Here, Wisdom calls: 'Seek Virtue first! be bold!
> As Gold to Silver, Virtue is to Gold.'
>
> (77-8)

Of course other people might think this rather odd, particularly those in the City:

> There, London's voice: 'Get Money, Money still!
> And then let Virtue follow, if she will.'
>
> (79-80)

And this allows a subtle change of direction; he is no longer writing about himself, but those other people. Retirement is forgotten and we very soon find ourselves faced again by a succession of pen portraits – Pope's favourite method of work and particularly of attack. Sir John Barnard, an MP and opponent of Walpole, was a man of such integrity he was admired by both political sides, but while he might abound in "spirit, sense and truth", without a personal fortune he could not expect to be rated in the eyes of the world. Wealth was what gave a man status, as it still does, no matter how dubiously it may have been acquired:

> Who counsels best? who whispers, 'Be but Great,
> 'With Praise or Infamy, leave that to fate;
> 'Get Place and Wealth, if possible, with Grace;
> 'If not, by any means get Wealth and Place.'
>
> (101-4)

Following Horace closely still, he shifts to a theme which had occupied him in the *Essay on Man* – inconstancy. We have Sir Jacob who sees Greenwich hill, declares there's no place on earth to match it, but before he's finished building he changes his mind:

> 'Away, away! take all your scaffolds down,
> 'For Snug's the word: My dear! we'll live in town.'
>
> (145-6)

The poor, Pope says, are no better, moving from one garret to another and even he himself is no different. He is slovenly in his dress (162) and his mind is in just as much a mess – neither of which statements rings true, but this is, we have to remember, a persona, not necessarily an autobiographical statement. And he ends by asking Bolingbroke to do something about it, to put him to rights, to make him the sort of man "whom Wisdom calls her own", but concludes by declaring himself a hopeless case.

It had been Bolingbroke, as Pope tells the story, who had first put to him the idea of imitating Horace. Visiting him once when Pope was unwell, Bolingbroke *happened* to take up a copy of Horace which lay on Pope's table, and *chanced* upon the First Satire of the Second Book and "observed how well that would fit my case, if I were to imitate it in English." It all sounds delightfully casual, especially Pope's claim that he "translated it in a morning or two". But whatever the truth, imitation did "hit his case" and not only the Satires.

The 'First Epistle' of Horace's Second Book was addressed to the Emperor Augustus who had asked for a poem to be dedicated to him, and it is clear that Horace admired both the man and his achievements. Conveniently, the full name of England's King, George II, for whom Pope had nothing but contempt, was George Augustus of Hanover, and so, in his Imitation Pope was able to lavish praise on him which he clearly did not mean and it is not until almost the end of the poem that we meet up with the line "Praise undeserv'd is Scandal in disguise." (413)

The "praise" certainly was undeserved. George II was a boor, with gross personal habits and a vile temper – he was even given to kicking people. He had no interest in the arts and even less in Pope. "Who is this Pope that I hear so much about?" he once asked. "I cannot discover what his merit is. Why will not my subjects write in prose?"

Pope's enjoyment of the 'parallels' can be seen in the opening sentence of the *Advertisement*: "The Reflections of *Horace*, and the Judgements passed in his Epistle to *Augustus*, seem'd so seasonable to the present times, that I could not help applying them to the use of my own Country." The irony – one could almost call it sarcasm – of Pope's praise is so cleverly done that neither the government nor the court could take any kind of proceedings against him without having to admit that the criticisms were true.

For example, the first three lines, closely following Horace, read:

> While You, great Patron of Mankind! sustain
> The balanc'd World, and open all the Main;
> Your Country, chief, in Arms abroad defend,
> (1-3)

and sound to be a genuine tribute, but when taken to refer to the contemporary situation the comparison is painful. The timorous foreign policy – as the Opposition saw it – of George II and Walpole meant that the Spanish *Main* was by no means open to British shipping and George had recently been absent so long in Hanover with his mistress, Amelie von Walmoden, that the *Arms* in this context are not even ambiguous. Yet how could the King really object to lines which described him as:

> Wonder of Kings! Like whom to mortal eyes
> None e'er has risen, and none e'er shall rise.
>
> (29-30)

At this point in the original Epistle, Horace, discursive as ever, asked how it was that if Rome's present leader exceeded all those of the past, why the ancient writers were held to be superior to the modern and Pope, following his lead, looks back over the history of English poetry, coming to the same conclusion – that it is illogical, as the ancients were modern once.

He is prepared to admit that far too much bad verse was being written:

> Now Times are chang'd, and one Poetic Itch
> Has seiz'd the Court and City, Poor and Rich:
>
> (169-70)

The dumbing-down of literature always raised his hackles and these lines do call to mind today's obsession with 'poetry workshops'. But he is very soon asserting the moral value of literature and so opposing George's contempt for it, but even among his more serious assertions he cannot deny himself a sly dig:

> What will a Child learn sooner than a Song?
> What better teach a Foreigner the tongue?
>
> (205-6)

An innocent sort of line until we realise that this foreign King could hardly speak a word of English and could not be bothered to learn.

In his praise of contemporary writers there is an unexpectedly warm tribute to Addison followed by a tribute to Swift which must have come close to sedition. "The Rights a Court attack'd, a Poet sav'd" is a reference to the scandal of 'Wood's halfpence' wherein a patent had been sold to circulate a debased copper currency in Ireland. It was Swift's opposition which had prevented it.

86

Turning to contemporary theatre, Pope ridicules the vacuous comedies, but puts some of the blame on the audience "the many-headed Monster of the Pit" (305) who, like Shakespeare's groundlings seem to been capable of nothing save "inexplicable dumb-shows and noise."

As the *Epistle* draws to a close Pope seems to be saying that he can understand why the King has so little patience with poets – they always want something a "place or pension from the Crown", but while pleading his own inability to sing the King's praises loud enough, so the flattery grows more and more extravagant and ironic until the hot-air balloon is punctured with that line so pointed and so finely ambiguous, "Praise undeserv'd is scandal in disguise".

All in all Pope wrote more than a dozen or so imitations or poems based on Horace, including an 'Epilogue to the Satires' which he first described as being "Something like Horace". It is a dialogue in which his *Friend* argues that Pope is not like Horace as Horace was more delicate and polite, and in this instance he is right. This is a bitter, outspoken and angry poem of protest and its personification of Vice is a clear foreshadowing of *The Dunciad*.

> Her Birth, her Beauty, Crowds and Courts confess,
> Chaste Matrons praise her, and grave Bishops bless;
> In golden Chains the willing World she draws,
> And hers the Gospel is, and hers the Laws,
> Mounts the tribunal, lifts her scarlet head,
> And sees pale Virtue carted in her stead!
> (145-50)

Dialogue II is much brighter in tone, and in the exchanges between Pope and his Friend it rattles along at a great pace. It is more assertive too:

> Ask you what Provocation I have had?
> The strong Antipathy of Good to bad.
> When Truth or Virtue an affront endures,
> Th' affront is mine, my Friend, and should be yours.
> (197-200)

And yet, looking back at the things to which Pope has felt this "strong Antipathy", we see that it included the lowering of literary standards, politicians who cheat and tell lies, corruption and bribery, the collapse of public and private morality, and obsession with money, vanity and materialism – and it seems that nothing has changed. There were, it seems, moments when Pope despaired and like Auden, in his poem on Yeats, admitted to himself that poetry "made nothing happen". In a footnote to the last line of this poem he wrote: "This was the last poem of the kind printed by our author, with a resolution to publish no more; but to enter thus, in the most plain and solemn manner he could, a sort of PROTEST against that insuperable corruption and depravity of manners, which he has been so unhappy as to live to see. Could he have hoped to have amended any, he had continued those attacks; but bad men were grown so shameless and so powerful, that Ridicule was become as unsafe as it was ineffectual."

9

The Dunciad

Published in 1743, *The Dunciad in Four Books* was Pope's last completed work, but, as we have seen, it had made its first appearance, as a poem in three books, as early as 1728 and was then directed primarily against Lewis Theobald. Theobald had had the temerity to publish *Shakespeare Restored; or, A Specimen of the many Errors, As Well Committed, as Unamended by Mr Pope in his late Edition of this Poet*, and the fact that much of his criticism had been valid did not make it any more palatable to Pope. He chose to dismiss it as a display of nit-picking pedantry and in 1729 confirmed this by bringing out a slightly longer version, *The Dunciad Variorum*, where the poem itself is almost swamped by a bogus 'scholarly' apparatus: page after page of 'Testimonials', copious footnotes, three separate introductions, seven appendices and two indexes. A joke, it has to be said, which is far too heavy-handed for us to be able to cope with today.

There is, however, in the account of the poem by *Martin Scriblerus*, one clear indication of its overall purpose. The action, he tells us, will be concerned with, "... the Removal of the Imperial seat of Dulness from the City to the polite world; as that of the Aeneid is the Removal of the empire of Troy to Latium." Leaving aside the comparison with *The Aeneid* for a moment, the references to the *City* and *the polite world* are crucial. They appear in the opening lines of the poem:

> The Mighty Mother, and her Son who brings
> The Smithfield Muses to the ear of Kings,
> I sing.

Smithfield was not only the centre of the London meat trade, it was also the site of the infamous Bartholomew Fair with all its low-life rough-and-tumble and debauchery, and the implication is that the *polite world*, which could once be counted on to uphold certain civilised standards, had succumbed to an invasion of dullness and trivia. In the eyes of Pope and his friends, they were living in a time of cultural crisis. *Martin Scriblerus* put it down to the fact that "Paper had become so cheap, and Printers so numerous, that a deluge of Authors covered the land." It is certainly true that a new class of readers had arisen, readers who by Pope's standards were barely literate, and they were being catered for by writers who themselves seemed ignorant of the great literary traditions which lay behind the peaks of 18th-century culture. It was the age of Grub Street and to Pope they *were* grubs and insects and they needed to be exterminated.

This was not a simple case of intellectual snobbery. Pope firmly believed that the debasement of literary standards inevitably brought with it a debasement of moral standards which, if allowed to go unchecked, would lead to a decline in the very fabric of civilised society itself. It was a cultural decay which he blamed on the House of Hanover, and as early as line 6 we find him asserting that "Dunce the second reigns like Dunce the first".

He was faced with a situation not unlike that where some of our own politicians have taken to claiming to be supporters of football clubs and fans of pop groups, thereby raising the spurious celebrity status of activities which are of very little real significance.

The references to *The Aeneid* should not be interpreted as a sign that *The Dunciad* is a mock-epic in the tradition of *The Rape of the Lock*, as far from being engaged in something inconsequential, the protagonists here are leading the country towards disaster. The echoes of epic which can be heard in the poem are meant to emphasise this and the term *anti-epic* might be more appropriate.

In the 1743 *Dunciad in Four Books*, Theobald was replaced as 'hero' by Colly Cibber, a far more noteworthy figure in every respect. An actor and playwright, he was also Poet Laureate – a political appointment more than an indication of any poetic ability. He had invited a degree of ridicule by writing an autobiography, something almost unheard of at the time, but it was his *Letter from Mr Cibber to Mr Pope* which earned him his place in *The Dunciad*. Pope had endured some scurrilous attacks in his time but this was special. Cibber claimed to have rescued Pope from a brothel. "I found this little hasty Hero, like a terrible *Tom Tit* pertly perching upon the Mount of Love! But such was my Surprize that I fairly laid hold of his Heels, and actually drew him down safe and sound from his Danger." There was even an illustration to go with it. Cibber was asking for trouble.

When we first encounter the Queen of Dulness she is in a "Cave of Poetry and Poverty", close to Grub Street, and also close to Bedlam, the notorious madhouse whose doorway was decorated with two grotesques depicting *Melancholy* and *Madness*. They had been sculpted by Cibber's father, and presented with such a gift Pope could not resist suggesting a family likeness:

> Where o'er the gates, by his fam'd father's hand
> Great Cibber's brazen, brainless brothers stand;
>
> (31-2)

It is doubtful whether anyone can ever have deliberately written a clumsier and uglier line. We do not need to have seen the statues; the words tell us what they were like.

It is the Day of the Lord Mayor's Show and the Queen casts her mind back over the names of the (dreadful) official poets who used to celebrate the Day until finally she thinks of the Laureate Cibber, here named as *Bays*. We are shown him in his study, trying to write, but at a loss for words. He sits surrounded by all his failed attempts:

> Round him much Embryo, much Abortion lay,
> Much future Ode, and abdicated Play.
>
> (121-2)

And so he builds an altar of 12 of the largest volumes on his shelves and burns his own work on it as an offering to the Queen, begging her to remember his lifelong service to her. In answer, she snuffs out the fire and transports him to her cave where he is anointed as her chosen son and in lines which parody Psalm 27:

> Lift up your Gates, ye Princes, see him come!
> Sound, sound ye Viols, be the Cat-call dumb!
>
> (301-2)

He is hailed as some kind of mock-messiah.

This was a notion which Pope took further in Book II. The second book of *Paradise Lost* had begun with Satan sitting:

> High on a throne of royal state, which far
> Outshone the wealth of Ormus or of Ind,

and in the clearest of echoes there is Cibber:

> High on a gorgeous seat, that far out-shone
> Henley's gilt tub, or Flecknoe's Irish Throne
> (1-2)

As an anti-hero he is now beginning to assume anti-epic proportions and the Queen announces that "high Heroic Games" are to be held in his honour. The first is a race between the publishers Lintot and Curll in pursuit of a phantom poet. "Huge Lintot" is no athlete, as Pope's description of his running style confirms:

> As when a dab-chick waddles thro' the copse
> On feet and wings, and flies, and wades, and hops;
> So lab'ring on, with shoulders, hands and head,
> Wide as a wind-mill all his figure spread,
> With arms expanded Bernard rows his state,
> (63-7)

Curll takes an early lead, but slips in a pool of excrement left in the road by one of his own female writers. Lintot overtakes him, but Jove, hearing Curll's pleas, intervenes and lets him win. The prize then disappears just as he reaches out to grasp it, but Dulness presents him with a tapestry as a consolation – a tapestry however which depicts a humiliating incident in his own life when the pupils of Westminster School tossed him in a blanket.

The next contest is to see who can piss the highest and "shameless Curll" wins this one easily with a jet like the river Po. The runner-up wins a chamber-pot. Then it is the poets' turn. Whoever can tickle (flatter) best will win a patron. Interestingly the victor this time is a young man who seems never to have written a poem at all, and he doesn't bother to offer his lordship any fulsome dedication either; he simply offers him his sister.

The poets are followed by the "chattering classes" and a "thousand tongues are heard in one loud din". As Maynard Mack has put it, there was "a new class of hack writers supplying an enlarging literate public with its daily fix of news, scandal, ballads, letters from a gentleman in the country to a gentleman in the city, pornographic novels, animadversions, humble addresses, sermons, dedications, invectives, and lampoons." It is this proliferation of Grub Street hacks which seems most to have aggravated Pope, that and the new breed of political journalist. For them the contest is to see who can dive deepest and stay submerged longest in the open sewer that was then the river Fleet, a contest which shows that mud-slinging and muck-raking have a long history in that particular profession. One of Walpole's chief spin-doctors, Jonathan Smedly, dives so deep the onlookers think he will never be seen again, but thanks to Mud-nymphs by the name of "Nigrina black and Merdamante brown" he resurfaces and is triumphant.

After contests for the publishers, the poets and the hacks, that only leaves the critics and they are challenged to stay awake during a reading of one of Sir Richard Blackmore's interminable epics. Of course they fail. They all fail. They fall asleep, along with the readers and everyone else present.

I have seen this part of *The Dunciad* hailed as evidence of Pope's 'comic genius', but it would be less than honest of me if I did not say that I do not find pissing contests and people diving into rivers of shit very amusing. It is not prudishness; it is that I feel such jokes are more the stock-in-trade of your average ten-year-old, along with farting. But at least they do give the lie to the old cliché about the 18th century being the *Age of Elegance*. There was as much silliness, smut and pornography in that century as in any other.

But why did Pope do it? Thinking back to 1728, he had been working for a decade and more on translating Homer, and as we have seen, he was very conscious of the linguistic decorum due to such an enterprise. Once he had finished, he maybe felt a sense of release and enjoyed indulging in a bout of the indecorous. Even if this is so, he still seems to me to have gone too far in the other direction.

When Book III opens, Cibber is lying with his head on the lap of Dulness and is fast asleep, but just as the epic hero Aeneas was taken to the Underworld to hear his father's prophecies of the future glory of Rome, so our anti-hero, in a dream, travels to the Elysian shade where, among the millions of dead poets waiting to return to earth in the form of a new book, he meets his guide and 'poetic father', Eklanah Settle, one of the last of the 'City Poets'. As Satan took Christ, so Settle takes Cibber to a mountain top from which he shows him Dulness' past 'glories': the burning of the greatest libraries of the world in China and Alexandria; the destruction of Rome by Visigoths and Huns; then papal Rome's stifling of science – "Her grey-haired Synods damning books unread" (102). And England itself overrun in the Middle Ages by monastic bigotry and religiosity.

'Behold yon Isle, by Palmers, Pilgrims trod,
Men bearded, bald, cowl'd, uncowl'd, shod, unshod,
Peel'd, patch'd, and pyebald, linsey-wolsey brothers,
Grave Mummers! sleeveless some and shirtless others,
That once was Britain.

(112-6)

All this was down to the credit of the Queen of Dulness, and greater glories yet, he predicts, are still to come, and while the long list of names that follows contains few which mean anything to us today, that may be the point – they always were and are nonentities. Cibber having been both playwright and actor, the theatre comes in for its share of ridicule.

Settle claims to have had some success in the establishment of Dulness in his own day, but Cibber, he is sure, will far outshine him. The omens, he says, look very auspicious. There is Pope's old adversary, Ambrose Philips, larded with well-paid public appointments, whereas John Gay, a founder member of the Scriblerus Club, was never granted any kind of political patronage; Swift, another Scriblerian, virtually banished to Ireland; and Pope too (in 1728) confined to translation for the past ten years. At this rate, he can look forward to the eventual collapse not only of educational establishments such as Eton and Westminster, but of Oxford itself. At this, the dream ends and Cibber wakes.

The final victory of the Queen of Dulness looks to be secure and in Book IV as she mounts her throne we see, bound and gagged and lying at her feet, her captives: science, wit, logic, rhetoric, morality, and of course "in ten-fold bonds the Muses lie". She looks to have conquered everywhere. As one might expect she does have a band of loyal cronies and the first to pay homage to her in "Harlot form" is Italian opera, an art form Pope dismissed in one of his footnotes for its "affected airs, its effeminate sounds". She comes to warn the Queen of a danger – Handel, whose oratorios were neither effeminate nor Italian. He has to be got rid of – to Ireland, where *The Messiah* had its first performance. Handel is a rare example of a creative artist who comes in for praise in *The Dunciad*.

Opera is soon followed by a crowd of other admirers, among whom a schoolmaster, Richard Busby of Westminster School, steps forward to assure the Queen that his pupils will never learn anything of significance and that he will keep on flogging them and making them uselessly recite things by rote. Any propensity to intellectual enquiry will be squashed:

> Whate'er the talents, or howe'er designed,
> We hang one jingling padlock on the mind.
>
> (161-2)

Dulness is delighted and wishes that the universities would follow suit, at which the pedant Richard Bentley, the Master of Trinity, who had "Made Horace dull, and humbled Milton's strains" speaks up and promises that he will deal with any outbreak of poetry:

> Turn what they will to Verse, their toil is vain,
> Critics like me shall make it Prose again.
>
> (213-4)

Bentley it was who had said of Pope's Homer, "It is a pretty poem, Mr Pope, but you must not call it Homer". That may have been two decades before, but revenge is a dish best served cold. But then

> In flow'd at once, a gay embroider'd race,
> And tittering pushed the Pedants off the place.
>
> (275-6)

It is a group of young aristocrats returned from the Grand Tour. They have gained nothing whatsoever by it and as his tutor says of one of them:

> Led by my hand, he saunter'd Europe round,
> And gather'd every Vice on Christian ground.
>
> (311-22)

Also among the crowd are two 'naturalists', one complaining that the carnation he has nurtured was trampled on by another chasing after a butterfly. The Queen praises them both as the trivialities they busy themselves with keep their thoughts off more serious things, such as God, and a cleric agrees:

> All-seeing in thy mists, we want no guide,
> Mother of Arrogance, and source of Pride!
> We nobly take the high Priori Road
> And reason downward, till we doubt of God.
>
> (469-72)

We should never doubt the gravity and seriousness of Pope's

concern. These dunces are, as he sees it, at the root of a decline not only of literature, but of morality and civilised life itself.

As the ceremonies come to a close the High Priest of Dulness offers a potion to all and sundry which deprives them of any mental faculties they may have and leaves them obsessed, as any young blood-about-town should be, with horse racing, hunting and their own foolish selves. The Queen then bids them all draw near so she can bestow titles and degrees upon them and with her own special blessing she adds:

> All my commands are easy, short and full:
> My sons! be proud, be selfish and be dull.
>
> (581-2)

And finally commands them to:

> MAKE ONE MIGHTY DUNCIAD OF THE LAND!
> (604)

She would have said more but a mighty yawn stopped her. It was a yawn which spread throughout the world. The poet asks his Muse to describe for him exactly what happened, but the Muse too "obeys the Pow'r" and is mute. Dulness is triumphant. Chaos and universal darkness reign once more and the poem ends with lines of the most threatening magnificence:

> No public Flame, nor private, dares to shine;
> Nor human Spark is left, nor Glimpse divine!
> Lo! thy dread Empire, CHAOS! is restor'd;
> Light dies before thy uncreating word:
> Thy hand, great Anarch! lets the curtain fall;
> And Universal Darkness buries All.
>
> (651-6)

And so Pope's poetry, which, like the Bible itself, began with a garden, ends with a city: from dreams of Eden to a vision of the Apocalypse. The young man who wrote *Windsor-Forest* and who looked around him with such confidence in the reign of Queen Anne, had come to view Georgian England with despair. And it is a despair which it is all too easy for us to comprehend when we consider our own tabloid press, not to mention the 'celebrity magazines', the state of our education system, the contempt some of our greedier politicians show for the electorate, the squalor of our towns and the rise of casual violence. Pope would do well to come back; we look to have a real and growing need of him.

And yet, was he right to feel such despair? Well, as far as literature is concerned, the answer would have to be: *not really*. Shortly after his death in 1744 – a peaceful death at Twickenham – Thomas Gray would publish that almost perfect poem *An Elegy Written in a Country Churchyard*, Christopher Smart would pen his ecstatic and exotic *A Song to David*, and then, at opposite ends of the country, two very different families – one in London and the other in the Lake District – both had baby boys who were christened William, and so, before the century was out, people were reading – even if as yet not actually appreciating – Wordsworth and Blake.

Bibliography

Editions:

The Poems of Alexander Pope edited by John Butt, 1963. (This is the reduced version of the six-volume Twickenham Text and is the edition used throughout this book)

Biographical/Critical:

Mavis Batey, *Alexander Pope: The Poet and the Landscape* (1999)
Laura Brown, *Alexander Pope* (1985)
Reuben A. Brower, *Alexander Pope: The Poetry of Allusion* (1959)
Peter Dixon, *Alexander Pope (Writers and their Background)* (1978)
Bonamy Dobree, *Alexander Pope* (1952)
Howard Erskine-Hill and Anne Smith, *The Art of Alexander Pope* (1979)
Howard Erskine-Hill, *The Life of Alexander Pope* (2008)
G. S. Fraser, *Alexander Pope* (1978)
Yasmine Gooneratne, *Alexander Pope* (1976)
Ian Gordon, *A Preface to Pope* (1976)
Ian Jack, *Augustan Satire* (1952)
Maynard Mack, *The Garden and The City* (1970)
Maynard Mack, *Alexander Pope: A Life* (1985)
Peter Quennell, *Alexander Pope: The Education of a Genius* (1968)
Pat Rogers, *The Alexander Pope Encyclopaedia* (2004)
Pat Rogers, *The Cambridge Companion to Alexander Pope* (2007)
R.W. Rogers, *The Major Satires of Alexander Pope* (1977)
Edith Sitwell, *Alexander Pope* (1930)
James Sutherland, *Preface to Eighteenth-Century Poetry* (1963)
Aubrey Williams, *Pope's* Dunciad (1955)

GREENWICH EXCHANGE BOOKS
STUDENT GUIDE LITERARY SERIES

The Greenwich Exchange Student Guide Literary Series is a collection of essays on major or contemporary serious writers in English and selected European languages. The series is for the student, the teacher and 'common readers' and is an ideal resource for libraries. The *Times Educational Supplement* praised these books, saying, "The style of [this series] has a pressure of meaning behind it. Readers should learn from that ... If art is about selection, perception and taste, then this is it."

(ISBN prefix 978-1-871551 applies unless marked*, when the prefix 978-1-906075 applies).

The series includes:

Antonin Artaud by Lee Jamieson (98-3)
W.H. Auden by Stephen Wade (36-5)
Honoré de Balzac by Wendy Mercer (48-8)
William Blake by Peter Davies (27-3)
The Brontës by Peter Davies (24-2)
Robert Browning by John Lucas (59-4)
Lord Byron by Andrew Keanie (83-9)
Samuel Taylor Coleridge by Andrew Keanie (64-8)
Joseph Conrad by Martin Seymour-Smith (18-1)
William Cowper by Michael Thorn (25-9)
Charles Dickens by Robert Giddings (26-9)
Emily Dickinson by Marnie Pomeroy (68-6)
John Donne by Sean Haldane (23-5)
Ford Madox Ford by Anthony Fowles (63-1)
The Stagecraft of Brian Friel by David Grant (74-7)
Robert Frost by Warren Hope (70-9)
Patrick Hamilton by John Harding (99-0)
Thomas Hardy by Sean Haldane (33-4)
Seamus Heaney by Warren Hope (37-2)
Joseph Heller by Anthony Fowles (84-6)
Gerard Manley Hopkins by Sean Sheehan (77-3)
James Joyce by Michael Murphy (73-0)
Philip Larkin by Warren Hope (35-8)
Laughter in the Dark – The Plays of Joe Orton by Arthur Burke (56-3)
George Orwell by Warren Hope (42-6)
Sylvia Plath by Marnie Pomeroy (88-4)

Poets of the First World War by John Greening (79-2)
Philip Roth by Paul McDonald (72-3)
Shakespeare's *A Midsummer Night's Dream* by Matt Simpson (90-7)
Shakespeare's *Hamlet* by Peter Davies (12-5)*
Shakespeare's *King Lear* by Peter Davies (95-2)
Shakespeare's *Macbeth* by Matt Simpson (69-3)
Shakespeare's *The Merchant of Venice* by Alan Ablewhite (96-9)
Shakespeare's *Much Ado About Nothing* by Matt Simpson (01-9)*
Shakespeare's Non-Dramatic Poetry by Martin Seymour-Smith (22-6)
Shakespeare's *Othello* by Matt Simpson (71-6)
Shakespeare's *Romeo and Juliet* by Matt Simpson (17-0)
Shakespeare's Second Tetralogy: *Richard II-Henry V*
by John Lucas (97-6)
Shakespeare's *Sonnets* by Martin Seymour-Smith (38-9)
Shakespeare's *The Tempest* by Matt Simpson (75-4)
Shakespeare's *Twelfth Night* by Matt Simpson (86-0)
Shakespeare's *The Winter's Tale* by John Lucas (80-3)
Tobias Smollett by Robert Giddings (21-1)
Alfred, Lord Tennyson by Michael Thorn (20-4)
Dylan Thomas by Peter Davies (78-5)
William Wordsworth by Andrew Keanie (57-0)
W.B. Yeats by John Greening (34-1)

FOCUS Series

Emily Brontë's *Wuthering Heights* by Matt Simpson (10-1)*
T.S. Eliot's *The Waste Land* by Matt Simpson (09-5)*
Thomas Hardy: *Poems of 1912-13* by John Greening (04-0)*
The Poetry of Ted Hughes by John Greening (05-7)*
George Eliot's *Middlemarch* by John Axon (06-4)*
Michael Frayn's *Spies* by Angela Topping (08-8)*
James Joyce's *A Portrait of the Artist as a Young Man*
by Matt Simpson (07-1)*
The Poetry of Tony Harrison by Sean Sheehan (15-6)*
Harold Pinter by Lee Jamieson (16-3)*
Wordsworth and Coleridge: *Lyrical Ballads (1798)*
by Andrew Keanie (20-0)*
Edward Thomas by John Greening (28-6)*
William Blake, *Songs of Innocence and Experience*
by Matt Simpson (26-2)*
F. Scott Fitzgerald's *The Great Gatsby* by Peter Davies (29-3)*